The Problem with Capital Punishment and Why It Should Be Abolished in America

The Problem with Capital Punishment and Why It Should Be Abolished in America

Vincent R. Jones Sr.

LEXINGTON BOOKS
Lanham • Boulder • New York • London

Published by Lexington Books
An imprint of The Rowman & Littlefield Publishing Group, Inc.
4501 Forbes Boulevard, Suite 200, Lanham, Maryland 20706
www.rowman.com

86-90 Paul Street, London EC2A 4NE

British Library Cataloguing in Publication Information Available

Library of Congress Cataloging-in-Publication Data

Names: Jones, Vincent R. Sr., author.
Title: The problem with capital punishment and why it should be abolished in America / Vincent R. Jones, Sr.
Description: Lanham : Lexington Books, 2023. | Includes bibliographical references and index. | Summary: "This book takes a harsh, critical look at capital punishment and points out the glaring flaws and misconceptions about its effectiveness. It makes a factual, legal, and moral argument for its abolition while refuting the main arguments in support of the death penalty" —Provided by publisher.
Identifiers: LCCN 2023039028 (print) | LCCN 2023039029 (ebook) | ISBN 9781666903829 (cloth) | ISBN 9781666903836 (epub)
Subjects: LCSH: Capital punishment—United States.
Classification: LCC KF9227.C2 J66 2023 (print) | LCC KF9227.C2 (ebook) | DDC 345.73/0773—dc23/eng/20230929
LC record available at https://lccn.loc.gov/2023039028
LC ebook record available at https://lccn.loc.gov/2023039029

For Justin, Vincent, Andrew, and in loving memory for my dad, Dorsey Allen Jones, the kindest and wisest man I have ever known. Sorely missed, never forgotten.

Contents

Preface

It was the Troy Davis case that did it for me. Prior to my deep dive into the facts of this case, I am ashamed to admit that my feelings about capital punishment were unreconciled at best, and ambivalent at worst. Prior to the Troy Davis case, I, like many Americans, felt that our death penalty administration was fairly implemented. I believed it was reserved for the worst of the worst offenders, and even they had the benefit of a series of appeals, where their innocence and constitutional rights could be protected against any substantive infringement. Then the Troy Davis case came to my attention. In a Constitutional Law class I was teaching, we decided to examine his case as an instructional exercise. The results of this one decision changed me forever.

It is because of this case that I uncovered the fact that claims of "actual" innocence are not welcome on appeal. It is because of this case that I discovered that far too many death row inmates are there in large part due to the incredible lack of legal representation they received from woefully inadequate court-appointed attorneys. It is because of the Troy Davis case that I began to pay attention to the growing number of innocent individuals who were exonerated from death row, often days, or even hours, before their impending executions. My deeper dive into this area revealed that the mentally ill, and the young, were more likely to confess to crimes they did not commit, and that far too often, these confessions would stand. Because of the Troy Davis case, my veil of ignorance was removed, and I could finally see what was truly happening on death rows around the country. It was not a pretty sight.

The Troy Davis case received worldwide attention, it became a *cause celebre*, and the calls to review his conviction became louder and louder as the clock moved closer to the appointed time of his execution. Mr. Davis maintained his innocence throughout. The only eyewitness who placed him at the scene of the admittedly horrible crime he was accused of, recanted her testimony; further, no physical evidence connected him to the crime, and no other witnesses appeared. His claim of actual innocence seemed ripe for Supreme Court intervention. I was so pleased to be right when on

Wednesday, September 21, 2011, the United States Supreme Court stayed the execution of Troy Davis. The news reached me just as I was walking into the Constitutional Law class where we were examining his case. I gleefully informed my students that despite flaws and errors, the system was working, and Mr. Davis's execution had been stayed.

We had a lively class discussion that evening, full of hypotheticals and case summaries. We effortlessly moved through the material I had set for us to examine, and the ninety-minute class ended swiftly. I issued new assignments, and after we said our goodbyes, I walked to my car, self-satisfied with my chosen profession. But when I turned on National Public Radio, I heard the broadcasted news that while I was in class, the Supreme Court had lifted the stay, and the State of Georgia hurriedly executed Troy Davis, in my view, to prevent any other challenges and to quiet the growing calls for a new trial. In less than ninety minutes, the Supreme Court had cleared the way, and his execution took place. His last words were haunting:

> *Well, first of all I'd like to address the MacPhail family. I'd like to let you all know, despite the situation—I know all of you are still convinced that I am the person that killed your father, your son and your brother, but I am innocent. The incident that happened that night was not my fault. I did not have a gun that night. I did not shoot your family member. But I am so sorry for your loss. I really am—sincerely. All I can ask is that each of you look deeper into this case, so that you really will finally see the truth. I ask my family and friends that you all continue to pray, that you all continue to forgive. Continue to fight this fight. For those about to take my life, may God have mercy on all of your souls. God bless you all.*[1]

After overcoming my deep disappointment in a legal system that would not grant a person the opportunity to prove his innocence, even in the face of what appears to be evidence of actual innocence, my class and I became advocates for the abolition of capital punishment as we petitioned the governor, who had already shown a lack of confidence in our death penalty system. He declared a moratorium in Illinois, largely based on the fact that he could not be sure that innocent people were not being executed. The failings of our criminal justice system in the area of capital punishment are horrifying. We have almost certainly executed an innocent person, and the likelihood of doing so continues as long as we have this form of punishment. Thurgood Marshall got it right in *Furman vs Georgia*, when he opined that the death penalty is unconstitutional under any circumstances.

I wrote this book because I did not want anyone else to be unaware of just how horribly ineffective, expensive, and morally reprehensible our capital punishment system is, and has been for quite some time. I wrote this book to advocate as well as inform. I wrote this book to pick up the mantle and do as Troy Davis asked with his dying last words, to "continue to fight this fight." After reading this book, I hope you will join me.

NOTE

1. "Troy Davis' Last Words Released by Georgia Department of Corrections," *Huffington Post*, October 7, 2011.

Acknowledgments

As a man of faith, it is important that I begin by thanking God for all the blessings I have received throughout my life, with the opportunity to write this book as one of the latest ones.

I would be less than respectful to go without recognizing Dr. James "Chip" Coldren, who not only gave me, an unproven professor, the opportunity to prove I could, but also mentored me and worked with me to produce an edited work as well as create new courses on Capital Punishment and Wrongful Convictions. This work would never have been possible without you, Chip, and I am eternally grateful.

To my friend and colleague Dr. Bruce Wilson, who pulled me aside one day when I was roaming the halls as an adjunct and convinced me that practicing law was not all I was meant to do, that there was a place for me in academia as well. Without your nudging me, I never would have considered becoming more than an adjunct. Thank you for guiding and mentoring me, for all the projects we have worked on together over the years, but most of all, for your genuine and true friendship.

To my sons, who inspire me each day to be a better version of myself, and to my loving wife, who is my rock and my oasis. Dot, I love you more than I have words to express.

Of course, none of this would have been possible without my great parents. My mother, Octavia, was my first educator; she opened a world of discovery for me when she took me to the library, got my first library card, and explained I could go anywhere and do anything by reading. The curiosity you inspired all those years ago still remains. My dad, Dorsey Jones, who left us in 2001 after a life well lived, told me from as far back as I can recall, "I will crawl so you can walk, I will walk so you can run, and I will run so you can soar!" Thank you, Dad; there is no one like you.

I must acknowledge the "angels of Franciscan hospital" in Olympia Fields—Dawn, Rachel, Crystal, Laurie, and Norma—who took such wonderful care of me as I dealt with my cancer treatments. You all made a difficult and frightening experience not only manageable, but pleasant and wholesome. Thank you for helping to save my life.

To Dr. Lance Wallace, my personal physician, who urged a very stubborn patient to go see a specialist because he did not like the results of some of my regular tests. Because of you, my cancer was caught early, and I am here today as a result. You literally saved my life.

My students are too numerous to name, but each one is a fundamental part of my development as a professor. Your questions and inquiries forced me to be my best, and for that I am truly grateful.

For my publishers and editors at Lexington Books, specifically Becca, Sara, and Emilia, who have demonstrated the patience of Job as I pushed my delivery dates further and further along the way, thank you for taking a chance on this first-time author and for all the mentoring along the way.

Lastly, in honor of my ancestors, who could not have imagined that their sacrifices, pain, suffering, and most importantly, faith would eventually produce me and my sons. I hope we are making you proud.

Introduction

It is undeniable that one of the most controversial issues in American law is the use of capital punishment as a punitive sanction in our criminal justice system. Since the inception of the death penalty in this country in 1608,[1] whether to continue to use execution as a form of punishment has been consistently and frequently debated.[2] Those in favor of the sanction have argued, *inter alia*, that it provides severe punishment for those who have committed severe crimes, and it is, therefore, a just and appropriate sanction.[3] Many have also taken the position that the use of this extreme form of punishment serves as a warning to others who may be inclined to commit similar crimes.[4] Furthermore, a consistent argument is that executing offenders who have committed horrible, often atrocious crimes provides victims and their families with closure.[5] Lastly, a prevailing argument, and one that seems to resonate with a large portion of the populace is that capital punishment is a necessary sanction, ostensibly reserved for the worst of the worst, and that without this threat of severity, chaos and lawlessness would ensue.

While all these arguments and more resonate with a large portion of the population, there is much more to this issue than the strictness of executing those who have run so far afoul of the law that society, through its criminal justice system, has determined that their actions have resulted in the forfeiture of their own lives. Many who oppose this form of punishment argue that the very nature of the punishment violates the Eighth Amendment's prohibition against cruel and unusual punishment.[6] That there are and have been, too many death-eligible crimes[7] that increase the prospects of execution.[8] It is also argued that the decision to execute a citizen, by the very government that exists to take care of and care for its citizenry, dehumanizes society as a whole and that the suggestion an execution provides some sort of closure for victims or acts as some form of a deterrent is patently false, and at the very least, cannot be proven.

If only capital punishment was as simple as the arguments outlined above. If only we could simply rely on public opinion exclusively and turn a blind eye to issues that go far beyond theories of "just deserts" and sympathetic arguments for the misbegotten criminal who has made one mistake too many.

But capital punishment is not a simple issue, and there is much more to the issue of capital punishment than weighing *pro* versus *con* arguments outlined above and throughout this book. As a nation, we have struggled with every aspect of the death penalty, from creating too many death-eligible offenses to how a capital trial should differ from other criminal trials, all the way to the method of execution. The method of execution has presented its own particular struggle as the search has moved the method from barbarism to seeking a more humane method of execution. In this country, we have used the following methods of execution over time:

1. Beheading
2. Pressing to death
3. Drawing and quartering
4. Breaking on the wheel
5. Drowning
6. Burning at the stake[9]
7. Hanging
8. Electrocution
9. Firing squad
10. Lethal gas
11. Lethal injection[10]

The struggle to find the appropriate method for legally taking the life of a citizen by its government strongly implies, albeit arguably, that perhaps this is not something that should ever be done. The fact is, there are many new and entirely compelling reasons why we, as a nation, must discontinue the use of capital punishment if we are to be who we purport to be—the leader of the free world. If we are to be the best version of ourselves, then there is no place for the death penalty in an enlightened society that recognizes the overwhelming futility and harm of capital punishment. As currently structured, maintaining a system of capital punishment is too costly, it is too often arbitrarily applied, and those needing representation the most—capital defendants—are too often represented by the worst and most unskilled lawyers.

These factors alone are enough to support the abolition of capital punishment in America, but there is one other factor that, in my view, should close the argument completely, for everyone involved. That factor is the existence of the very real possibility of executing the innocent. We can no longer be satisfied with a criminal justice system that brings with it a significant possibility of committing the greatest injustice of all: executing an innocent person. It has been done before, and as long as we continue to administer this form of punitive sanction, it is very likely to happen again.[11] It is universally accepted that the type and quality of judicial review afforded to death penalty defendants and their cases is woefully inadequate to prevent the execution of some prisoners who were wrongfully convicted and later sentenced to death.[12]

Continuing to administer a system that includes capital punishment can no longer be a neutral issue. We can no longer treat this issue as an intellectual exercise of pro and con arguments. Innocent lives are literally at stake, and I would argue the soul of our nation is equally at stake. Since the end of World War II, the United States has taken up the mantle of being the moral conscience of the world and the protector of international human rights. We cannot continue to cast ourselves as a great nation cognizant of individual rights, liberties, and freedoms with the moral stain of an unjust and inequitable system of capital punishment on our collective consciences. Nor can we continue to be the model of blind, fair, and impartial justice to ourselves and the world with the continuation of this very clear injustice. Our neighbors to the north, Canada, and the South, Mexico, not only have outlawed this form of punishment in their countries, but will also refuse to extradite any criminal from their lands unless there are assurances that upon their delivery to the United States, the death penalty is not an option for punishment—regardless of the crime that was committed. Throughout the whole of Europe, only one country still allows the death penalty as a punitive sanction.[13] We cannot in good conscience continue to ignore the facts, supplant them with inflamed rhetoric, or maintain tough policies designed to incite public fear and support but fail to address the real problems.

Public support for the continued use of the death penalty has been consistently waning. In 2019, a Gallup poll was taken, in which 60 percent of the people polled supported a life sentence over the death penalty being imposed. Conversely, only 36 percent supported the use of the death penalty, with 4 percent undecided.[14] The time to abolish capital punishment in every state, district, territory, and province of the United States has come. This book presents, in no uncertain terms, the reasons why.

NOTES

1. It is believed that the first person to be legally executed in the United States was Captain George Kendall. Historical records reveal he was a councilor for the colony of Virginia who was tried, convicted, and executed for the crime of espionage, spying for the country of Spain. See *Part 1: History of the Death Penalty*, Death Penalty Info. Center, http://www.deathpenaltyinfo.org/part-i-history-death-penalty (last visited March 1, 2020); see also Michael H. Reggio, *History of the Death Penalty*, in Society's Final Solution: A History and Discussion of the Death Penalty 3 (Laura E. Randa ed., 1977).

2. See, e.g., Symposium, *The Future of the Death Penalty in America*, 67 U. Miami. L. Rev. 329 (2013).

3. See, infra, Part IV.B.

4. See, infra, Part IV.A.

5. See, infra, Part IV.C.

6. U.S. Const. amend VIII.

7. A death penalty–eligible crime is a crime that, once committed, and after having been found guilty of the commission of said crime, the accused is "eligible" for the pronouncement of a death sentence, depending upon the decision of the judge or jury. (For a list of federal offenses punishable by death, see 41 Federal Capital Offenses, PROCON, http://www.deathpenalty.procon.org/view.resource.php?resourceID=004927 [last visited August 15, 2015]).

8. See Vincent R. Jones, and Bruce Wilson, *Innocence and Its Impact on the Reassessment of the Utility of Capital Punishment: Has the Time Come to Abolish the Ultimate Sanction?* 67 U. Miami L. Rev. 459, 464–66 (2013); see also "The Death Penalty in California: Cruel and Unusual, Judge Strikes a Blow against Capital Punishment," *Economist* (Jul. 26, 2014), http://www.economist.com/news/united-states/21608773-judge-strikes-blow-against-capitalpunishment-cruel-and-unusual.

9. This particular form of cruelty was primarily reserved for slaves who killed their masters or participated in the planning of a slave revolt. See Bohm, *Death Quest III*, 145.

10. See Bohm, *Death Quest III,* 145.

11. For a list of individuals who were executed but very likely innocent, see Death Penalty Info Center, *Executed but Possibly Innocent*, https://www.deathpenaltyinfo.org/executed-but-possibly-innocent.

12. Ibid.

13. There are forty-four countries in Europe, and Belarus is the only one that still allows capital punishment. It is carried out by firing squad.

14. See Death Penalty Information Center, *Public Opinion Polls.*

Chapter 1

The History of the Death Penalty in America: A Brief Overview

In order to understand how we arrived at this moment in time, it is important to begin with a historical perspective. The first person to be legally executed in the United States, at that time known as the colonies, was Captain George Kendall.[1] Ironically, Kendall was not executed for murder, felony murder, or any of the major crimes that we have executed so many for over the decades; Captain George Kendall's crime was spying on the United States for Spain. His execution was carried out by firing squad in 1608. This method is still a military option available today.

The early colonists came to America armed with the experiences of eighteenth-century Europe, where capital punishment was widely used.[2] In England, for example, the death penalty was imposed for a variety of offenses, and that tradition continued in the New World. In America in the early 1600s, death-eligible offenses included: trading with the indigenous people, stealing grapes, idolatry, witchcraft, blasphemy, murder, poisoning, bestiality, adultery, sodomy, serving as a false witness in capital cases, conspiracy, and rebellion.[3] The large number of death-eligible crimes reflected the puritanical view of the times, which intertwined crime with sin.[4]

The methods of execution also reflected the harshness of the times; rather than rehabilitation and humane treatment of the condemned, the emphasis was on punishment and atonement. Early executions were a community event and often took on a "carnival-like" atmosphere. Families brought their children to witness the event and to listen to the local religious leader preach about sin and attempt to save the soul of the condemened. Often a procession, including the accused, the local religious leader, law enforcement officers, and the judges or magistrate, would march through the town, eventually reaching the gallows, where the execution would occur. It was typical for the condemned to be allowed to speak his/her last words. In some instances, the sincerity of the words of the condemned, particularly when contrition was evident, could persuade the executioner to forego the execution altogether.[5]

MODERN DEATH PENALTY ADMINISTRATION AND LAW

In the United States, the use of capital punishment marched forward uninterrupted and primarily unquestioned until the early 1970s. However, long before the 1970s, questions about the morality of its use began to rise in earnest—as early as the mid-1700s. In fact, one of the first persons to publicly organize against its use was Dr. Benjamin Rush, a Philadelphia-based physician (and one of the original signers of the Declaration of Independence).[6] Dr. Rush, along with several prominent society members and Quakers, organized abolitionist movements to end the use of capital punishment in America. Early death-penalty abolitionists often joined their cause with slave abolitionists and women's suffragists. These abolitionist societies were most active along the Eastern seaboard.[7]

From these early efforts to abolish capital punishment, the abolitionist movement grew increasingly critical of the continued use of this criminal sanction. Notwithstanding this growing criticism, public support for its use remained consistently favorable. However, this all changed in 1972, when the United States Supreme Court, spurred by Justice Thurgood Marshall, in *Furman versus Georgia*, declared that the death penalty constituted cruel and unusual punishment and was therefore prohibited by the Eighth Amendment to the United States Supreme Constitution. This Prohibition was short-lived, however, because the same Supreme Court clarified, a mere four years later in *Gregg versus Georgia*, that the death penalty, in and of itself, did not necessarily constitute cruel and unusual punishment. The death penalty, therefore, was reinstated by the Court, and it has continued undisturbed until today.[8]

WHY DO WE CONTINUE TO HAVE A DEATH PENALTY IN AMERICA?

The inevitable questions that are often asked are: Why do we have a death penalty in America? What purpose is it intended to serve? Does it accomplish its intended goals? After consideration, there appear to be three principal theories that continue to endorse and support the continued use of this form of punishment, which include: deterrence, retribution, and closure for the victims or their families.

DETERRENCE

One of the arguments in support of continuing the use of the death penalty is the deterrence theory of punishment. It is posited that in order to prevent the rampant commission of violent crimes, an equally harsh penalty must be used to deter or influence others from committing the same or similar offenses.[9] Therefore, vicious crimes must be met with harsh penalties—and the harshest of them all is the execution of the offender. Knowing that death-eligible offenses will be met with the death penalty is an important factor in controlling crime and criminals, according to the deterrence theory of punishment.

RETRIBUTION

Another leading theory in support of capital punishment is requisite punishment, or retribution. As this theory suggests, extreme offenses must be met with equally extreme punishment.[10] It is only in this manner that society maintains its "balance." Offenders must be punished for the commission of their crimes to prevent societal imbalance. This theory goes to our base instinct most often exemplified by the biblical phrase "an eye for an eye."[11] The "eye for an eye" philosophy has permeated the use of the death penalty and still carries considerable weight in the modern discussion of its use.[12]

CLOSURE FOR VICTIMS

A third, and initially persuasive theory in support of capital punishment is the theory that executing the offender provides badly needed closure for the victims. As this theory goes, once a capital crime is committed, capital punishment provides two important benefits: law and order, and closure or an end to the trauma. To accomplish these two goals, the offender must be punished to assuage the hurt of victims and their families and to provide the consistency of law and order. It is argued that victims cannot have closure until the appropriate punishment has been meted out and that society benefits from this final act of justice by seeing that law and order prevails.

On the surface, all these theories seem applicable to capital punishment, but upon closer examination, we find that each theory necessarily fails. Let's take a closer look at these theories, one by one, and see if they, in fact, accomplish their intended goals.

DETERRENCE: DOES THE DEATH PENALTY ACTUALLY DETER CRIME?

A common belief among death-penalty proponents is that capital punishment deters crime. The theory is that those who commit a death-eligible offense will observe the harshness of the punishment imposed upon the convicted and will independently decide it is best that the would-be offender refrain from committing such a crime, lest they, too, suffer this harsh fate. The problem is that such a theory presupposes that capital offenders take the time to consider the consequences of their actions before acting and weighs the likelihood of having to bear these consequences. The truth is, most offenders simply never consider getting caught and therefore this intellectual exercise, of considering whether to act or not, is never a part of the ultimate equation. Getting caught is never part of the plan; therefore, suffering the consequences of getting caught is equally not part of the plan.

To this point, Marshall Dayan, an assistant professor of law at North Carolina Central University, argues that murderers do not consider the penalty for their crimes because they do not expect to get caught; thus, the death penalty has no deterrent effect. Further, he suggests that the underpinnings of the deterrence theory is also flawed in that it relies on the proposition that individuals know the harshness of the penalty for their crime before they commit it. However, Dayan points out that several members of law enforcement, lawyers, and even judges have been found guilty of committing murder at one time or another, notwithstanding the fact that they are fully aware and have been trained to understand the harshness of the penalty before they commit murder—yet many still do.[13]

To illustrate this point, he uses the case of William Huggins Jr., a former assistant district attorney prosecuted for soliciting murder. As a prosecutor, Huggins had intricate and specific knowledge of the consequences of and penalty for murder, but even though he was armed with this specific knowledge of the penalty and consequences, it did not prevent him from conspiring to commit murder.[14] Or, for example, take the case of prominent South Carolina attorney Alex Murdaugh, now convicted of the double murder of his wife and son, presumably to hide his financial crimes. Murdaugh knew very well the consequences of his actions, yet he was not deterred notwithstanding this knowledge.[15]

In order for the deterrence theory to work, we must assume the general public, including potential criminals, would be deterred from committing death-eligible offenses simply from prior knowledge of the punishment before the crime is committed. We must assume that potential criminals would know and understand the penalty for their actions before they commit them and that this knowledge would deter them from committing their crimes. History and experience inform us that this supposition is false.

But let's not stop here. Let's also consider the class and type of criminals for which no amount of prior knowledge will deter them from their crimes. These are the people who commit crimes as part of a self-imposed mission or those who operate from a compulsion. Even if we could rely on rational thought by potential capital offenders as a reason to continue support capital punishment, the deterrence theory fails to consider these type of offenders—who will never be deterred by the penalty associated with the crime. For example, consider serial killers, who act out of a depraved mental compulsion; attention-seeking killers, who kill for the notoriety; suicidal killers, who kill to be killed due to their desire to commit suicide but lack of ability to do it themselves; or the domestic terrorist, who kills based upon a perceived grievance or slight with the full intention of self-executing once their targets have been hit. These are all examples of the types of capital offenders who would not be affected by the harshness of the penalty for their actions. In fact, in certain circumstances, many would embrace it as part of their perceived martyrdom.[16]

Finally, assuming that having a death penalty would, in fact, serve as a deterrent, then states *with* a death penalty should be able to demonstrate a lower murder rate[17] than states *without* a death penalty. However, according to the Death Penalty Information Center, states that have abolished the death penalty, such as North Dakota, Maine, Rhode Island, and Minnesota, have lower murder rates than states that continue to allow the death penalty, including Alabama, Tennessee, Louisiana, and the state with the most executions—Texas.[18]

Based upon the foregoing, and existing research, there seems to be no relationship between the harshness of the penalty and its deterrence to crime. Simply stated, it does not appear that having the death penalty available as a punitive sanction acts as an effective deterrent to the commission of death-eligible offenses by would-be offenders.

DOES THE EXECUTION OF AN OFFENDER PROVIDE CLOSURE TO VICTIMS?

One of the leading arguments in favor of continuing capital punishment is that it provides closure for victims. The argument asks, "What about the victims and co-victims of these capital offenders? Shouldn't the death penalty exist to provide them with a sense of finality and closure, putting an end to their misery and loss?" Perhaps Professor Thomas Bretonneau,[19] a staunch conservative and white nationalist who supported capital punishment, captured the victim's-need-for-closure sentiment best:

> The Justice that the death penalty seeks, it seeks foremostly for the deceased, who can no longer demand it for himself. In another way, the death penalty is society's belated application of self-defense in place of the victim. "We should have liked to have been there," the sentence says, "to have met lethal force with lethal force for the victim's sake." The death thus honors and commemorates the dead and speaks to the sanctity of life in the civilized order.[20]

Contrary to this sentiment, most victims allege that the execution of the offender does nothing to assuage the loss; in fact, many take the position that executions continue the process of needlessly punishing innocent families, including the families of the offender. An even more interesting point of view is the one offered by Marietta Jaeger Lane, whose daughter was kidnapped and murdered. When asked about her view of the death penalty, Jaeger Lane said:

> Loved ones wrenched from our lives by violent crimes deserve more beautiful, noble memorials than premeditated, state-sanctioned killings.[21]

Or consider the view of Vicki Scheiber, whose daughter Shannon was murdered: "In honor of our daughter, my husband and I are committed to spending the remainder of our lives trying to seek not just the elimination of the death penalty, but meaningful change."[22] Still others take a less-charitable position against the death penalty, arguing that murderers should live and suffer so they can think about the harm they have caused.

Does the execution of offenders provide closure for the victims and victims' families? Arguably not.[23]

Capital punishment is not a single-issue problem. It is not as simple as determining whether we should use it or not. This particular issue goes much further than that, and in the coming chapters, we will see that not only is capital punishment ineffective, but it is horribly misplaced and tremendously negative for our criminal justice system and for this country.

NOTES

1. Robert M. Bohm, *Death Quest III* (2007), 1. See also *History of the Death Penalty*, Death Penalty Information Center, http://www.deathpenaltyinfo.org/part-i-history-death-penalty (last visited March 1, 2020); see additionally Michael H. Reggio, "History of the Death Penalty," in *Society's Final Solution: A History and Discussion of the Death Penalty 3*, Laura E. Randa, ed., cram.com.

2. See Bohm, supra note 1. See also Reggio, supra note 1.

3. Ibid. See generally 1–12.

4. Robert Bohm, *Death Quest III: An Introduction to the Theory and Practice of Capital Punishment in the United States*, Pamela Chester et al., eds., 4th ed. (Boston: Anderson Publishing, 2012).

5. Ibid. at 2 ("Condemned prisoners would often . . . confess their guilt and proclaim their newfound faith to the congregation and especially its most influential members [because it gave the] prisoner their best opportunity of receiving executive clemency.")

6. See generally, ibid., at 6–7, discussing the period between 1825 and 1850 as a time of reform in America when the "general abolitionist sentiment, spurred anti-death penalty activity."

7. Ibid., at 5–7.

8. Some states, however, have placed limits on the death penalty or stricken it down completely. See "States with and Without the Death Penalty," Death Penalty Information Center, http://www.deathpenaltyinfo.org/states-with-and-without-deathpenalty (last visited August 16, 2015).

9. "Deterrence: In Support of the Death Penalty," Death Penalty Curriculum, http://deathpenaltycurriculum.org/student/c/about/arguments/argumentla.htm (last visited August 15, 2015).

10. See "Retribution: In support of the Death Penalty," Death Penalty Curriculum, http://deathpenaltycurriculum.org/student/about/c/arguments/argument (last visited August 15, 2015).

11. Holy Bible, Deuteronomy 19:21 (King James Version).

12. See, e.g., Art Swift, "Americans: 'Eye for An Eye' Top Reason for Death Penalty," Gallup (Oct. 23, 2014), http://www.gallup.com/poll/178799/americans-eye-eye-top-reasondeathpenalty.aspx ("Americans who favor the death penalty most often cite 'an eye for an eye' as the reason they hold their position, with 35% mentioning it."); "Retribution: In Support of the Death Penalty," supra note 30 ("Retribution has its basis in religious values, which have historically maintained that it is proper to take an 'eye for an eye' and life for a life.").

13. See Marshall Dayan, "Death Penalty No Deterrent, Even to an Assistant Prosecutor," *Herald Sun*, Sept. 24, 2002, at A13 ("A former client of mine, a convicted murderer, once said, 'You can tell people that you are going to boil 'em in hot oil, but it won't deter crime, because criminals don't think they are going to get caught.'"); see also Lauri S. Friedman, *The Death Penalty* (New York: Greenhaven Press, 2006).

14. Ibid.

15. See Elizabeth Campbell, CBS News, "Alex Murdaugh trial: As prosecution rests in double murder case, here's where things stand," cbsnews.com (retrieved on February 19, 2023).

16. See Bohm, supra note 14, at 164–65.

17. Murder rate was chosen for comparison as it is the principal crime universally deemed to merit the imposition of capital punishment.

18. See Murder Rates Nationally and by State, *Death Penalty Information Center*, http://www.deahtpenaltyinfo.org/murder-ratesnationally-and-state (last visited August 8, 2015).

19. Dr. Thomas F. Bertonneau was a conservative author and professor who taught at several institutions and was a member of the English Faculty at SUNY Oswego. He had significant ties to white nationalism, and his articles and essays appeared in white nationalist publications. He was in favor of capital punishment.

20. Thomas F. Bertonneau, *Execution Gives Justice to the Forgotten Victim*, Benighted Comment (2001), http://nenightedcomment.com/essays/execution-gives-justice-to-the-forgotten-victim.

21. See "Victims and the Death Penalty," Death Penalty Information Center, http://www.deathpenaltyinfo.org/victims-death-penalty (last visited August 15, 2015).

22. "Victims and the Death Penalty, Testimony in Support of Senate Bill 820," Vicki A Scheiber.

23. See Catherine Appleton and Bent Grover, "The Pros and Cons of Life Without Parole," 47 *Brit. J. Criminological*, 597.

Chapter 2

The Death Penalty: An Unjust and Arbitrarily Applied Penalty

We have already discussed the fact that there are deeper issues with the issue of capital punishment beyond the basic question of whether you are for it or against. In my view, there are questions that supersede the "for or against" arguments, questions that must be resolved before one can decide whether they are pro or con capital punishment. For example, when it comes to punishment, every right-thinking person would want all punishment to be doled out fairly. Even a small child will cry out in protest if they perceive to be on the receiving end of an unfair punishment. Certainly, the least that we should expect from a death sentence is that the decision has been reached fairly and that the sentence is equally administered to all offenders. This is clearly not too much to ask of a criminal justice system that purports to administer blind justice, giving no special favors or treatment. This is a very lofty theory, but obviously, we all know this is not true. It should come as no surprise that it is not true when it comes to the ultimate sanction either.

The fact is, the death penalty is arbitrarily applied and arbitrarily enforced in several ways. It is geographically arbitrary, it is economically arbitrary, it is arbitrary based upon who the victim is,[1] and "finally, it is arbitrary in the most basic sense—it is ultimately within the jury's, [or judge's], discretion to impose the death penalty or not, and [they] need not explain the basis of their decision. A judge or jury may grant mercy to one defendant, but not to another for whatever reason [they] see fit."[2]

Simply put, whether a defendant is charged under a death-penalty statute and sentenced to death too often has more to do with nonlegal factors than with the crime committed, and the defense undertaken. The inherent unfairness of capital punishment finally came to the forefront in a legendary Supreme Court case, *Furman versus Georgia*. When the United States Supreme Court decided to abolish capital punishment in *Furman versus Georgia* in 1972,[3] it did so primarily on three particularly important grounds:

1. That the cruelness of the sanction was so harsh that it violated the Eighth amendment's constitutional prohibition against cruel and unusual punishment,
2. That the use of capital punishment was too arbitrarily enforced, and
3. That the application of capital punishment was too discriminatorily applied to be maintained as an equitable legal sanction.

In this case, the court zeroed in on the inescapable truth, that the death penalty was arbitrary and discriminatory, while also violative of the Eighth Amendment. In fact, it is very possible that an individual who commits a crime in one state will not be executed or even eligible for capital punishment, while in another state, a person committing the same crime will be subjected to the death penalty. A clear example of this are the death-penalty statutes in the states of Illinois and Indiana. Two similarly situated midwestern states, literally right next to each other, are demographically similar in many respects, yet one has the death penalty, and the other does not. The same can be said of Ohio and Michigan, or Iowa and Missouri. In each instance, these states are similarly situated; are very near, if not adjacent to each other; and have similar population sizes and very similar crime rates. Yet one executes, and the other does not. In fact, the use of the death penalty appears to have no statistical bearing on the commission of a death-eligible crime, but rather, it falls with more certainty based upon the location of the crime.

Upon closer examination, we see that when it comes to the application of capital punishment, there are wide variances in who does, and does not, receive the death penalty. These variances can include age, gender, geography, the race of the defendant, and the race of the victim, and some would argue that even the economy influences this particular outcome. All these statistical, biographical, nonlegal factors are significant in some areas, but they absolutely should play no role in who receives the death penalty and who does not.

The fact is, any system that produces such a final sanction that is so clearly affected by so many nonlegal arbitrary factors should not continue to exist in a fair and equitable criminal justice system. Why does such arbitrary application exist? It is not difficult to find the sources of arbitrariness; it can be traced to a variety of sources, such as:

- Statutes that justify arbitrariness due to lack of choice.
- Jurors' misunderstanding of sentencing obligations and confusing instructions.
- Rule changes by the Supreme Court.
- Problems defining "murderous intent" or "premeditation."[4]
- The availability, and the discretionary use, of plea bargains.

- Inconsistent rulings from various appellate courts.

GEOGRAPHY

One of the most obvious arbitrary factors is geography. When we examine the states that continue to maintain capital punishment, we see that the locus of the crime is a particularly important factor in determining who is executed and who is not. You will note that the majority of the states that continue to execute defendants are located in the South. In fact, the leading states (Texas, Georgia, Louisiana, Virginia, Florida) are all southern states, with Virginia having the distinction of being the fastest to execute, Florida the slowest, and Texas the most voluminous. There is no legal factor that would make death eligibility more prevalent in the South over Northern states, yet this singular arbitrary fact can have a tremendous impact on who lives and who dies. We also see that even intrastate, the southern or rural portion of a state (e.g., Illinois before capital punishment was abolished) produced more death sentences than in the more northern or urban portions of the state. A distance of a few miles can determine whether a person lives or is executed in our system of justice. No equitable criminal sanction should be so greatly affected by geography.

DEATH BY JURISDICTION

- There are twenty-five states and the federal government where executions are legal.
- Twenty-two states have abolished the death penalty.
- Three states have governor-imposed moratoriums.
- The District of Columbia abolished capital punishment.
- More than 80 percent of post-*Furman* executions have been in Southern states.

The death penalty, largely due to jurisdictional differences, has become a product of chance rather than a soberly considered and equally applied legal sanction. Some jurisdictions have the reputation of being "hanging counties" (for example, Dallas County, Texas), and some juries have the reputation of being "hanging juries," wherein the outcome is predetermined. Further, some years, due to external conditions, appear to be "hanging years."[5] The table below shows the variance in the number of executions each year in the United States since 2013.

Table 2.1: Number of Executions Per Year

2020	3
2019	9
2018	13
2017	7
2016	20
2015	28
2014	35
2013	39
2014	35
2013	39

Source: Death Penalty Information Center. Death Penalty Information Center (DPIC) Fact Sheet, Facts about the Death Penalty, last updated July 17, 2023, https://www.deathpenaltyinfo.org, last retrieved July 19, 2023.

There are some general facts we can extrapolate from the data that offer a sobering insight into how random the year, and the jurisdiction, may affect the number of executions. For example:

a. The farther North a death-eligible crime is committed, the less likely the death penalty will be imposed.
b. Rural areas impose the death penalty more often than urban areas.
c. The state of Texas executes the largest number of people virtually every year.
d. For every person executed, there is someone else who committed a worse crime and received a life sentence.

VIRGINIA AND CAPITAL PUNISHMENT

At the time I was writing this chapter on the arbitrary nature of the application of capital punishment, some startling news, or "Breaking News," appeared over the airwaves of National Public Radio with this headline: "Virginia Governor Signs Law Abolishing the Death Penalty." The seismic reverberations through the world of capital punishment for those in favor and against could not be larger and more earth-shattering.

On Wednesday, March 24, 2021, Democratic Governor Ralph Northam signed a bill into law abolishing the death penalty in the state of Virginia. This action followed the legislature's actions, which passed the measure in February. Governor Northam is quoted as saying:

> *It is the moral thing to do to end the death penalty in the Commonwealth of Virginia. Virginia will join twenty-two other states that have ended use of the*

death penalty. This is an important step forward in ensuring that our criminal justice system is fair and equitable to all.[6]

Virginia is the first state in the South to abolish capital punishment. Given that state's history, this is a fact of noteworthy significance. Historically, Virginia has executed more people than any other state, since the first execution in Jamestown in 1608. When determining it was time to abolish capital punishment in this state, those supporting the abolition cited several significant factors upon which the decision in favor of abolition was based: 1) the high cost of maintaining capital punishment as a sanction; 2) the possibility of executing the innocent; and 3) the disproportionate racial impact and its over application to Black defendants, especially when their victims were White.

The death penalty is the direct descendant of lynching. It is State-sponsored racism, and we have an opportunity to end this today.—Delegate Jay Jones (speaking on the House floor)[7]

TEXAS AND CAPITAL PUNISHMENT

It would be a dereliction if special attention were not paid to Texas and its use and administration of capital punishment. This is not a compliment. Year in and year out, Texas leads the nation with the number of individuals who are executed. Along with this horrible distinction, we can find virtually every form of abuse in the Texas system of capital punishment. Wrongful convictions are rampant, and examples of the worst capital-defense lawyers are so extreme that it is literally hard to believe as true. Rogue prosecutors intentionally prosecute the innocent, or at the very least, turn a blind eye to suspicious evidence and facts, and law enforcement investigators have engaged in some of the most reprehensible misconduct. From 1976 through 2020, the state of Texas has executed five times as many people (569) as the second-place state (Virginia with 113) and over fifteen times as many as the number-ten state (Arizona with 37). There are geographical and cultural differences in Texas that can help explain some of this, but it is much deeper than culture and geography. Having defended individuals in Texas, I can clearly see the contrast between how criminal law is practiced in my home city, Chicago, and what I experienced in Dallas County, and it was shocking and unparalleled. I experienced a callousness to protecting the rights of defendants in Texas that I did not experience in any other jurisdiction.[8] The intersection of race, culture, immigration, poverty, crime, and a very rigid power structure (characterized by the "good old boy" network) produces some very horrible results for the vulnerable in the Texas criminal justice system. An example of this philosophy is evident in a statement made by Texas Representative Chip

Roy during an anti-Asian–violence hearing after the tragic murders of eight Asian Americans by a twenty-one-year-old white male gunman in Georgia. Roy said, "We believe in justice. There are old sayings in Texas about find all the rope in Texas and get a tall oak tree. We take justice very seriously. And we ought to do just that. Round up the bad guys. That's what we believe."[9]

Why do capital murder cases proceed through the Texas State Court System with a speed unimaginable in other parts of the country? Brent Newton, in his article on capital punishment, notes that there are criminal justice legal procedures, unique to only Texas, that enable the state of Texas to execute convicted murderers with astonishing frequency and at an arguably rapid pace. These unique procedures are:

1. Texas appellate judges are elected rather than appointed. As such, their decisions must appease the public's get-tough-on-crime perspective if they ever hope to be elected or reelected. Newton claims these elected judges do not carefully consider the complexities of each specific case. As evidence, he claims, "During the past few years, the Texas Court of Criminal Appeals has refused to publish most of its decisions in death penalty cases, including many cases that discuss important issues of first impression. Often these opinions take positions entirely inconsistent with prior decisions by the court and fail to mention the legal conflict. He goes on to add that "generally speaking, there is a hit-and-mostly-miss quality in the Court of Criminal Appeals' death penalty decisions." He goes on to say that "Only a few judges . . . have been capable of or willing to write scholarly decisions, whether granting or denying relief."
2. Texas does not have a public defender system for indigent defendants. Instead, they rely upon court-appointed lawyers who often do not have any experience with capital-murder defenses or appeals. Stories of incompetent defenses in capital-cases counsel are legion in Texas. In one striking appellate decision, the appellate court, while turning down a habeas appeal based upon incompetent defense counsel, concluded that "the Constitution does not say that the lawyer has to be awake during trial proceedings."
3. Until the early 1990s, Texas did not permit jurors to adequately consider mitigating evidence in the sentencing phase of a trial. As a result, there are many people on death row who possibly would not be there had evidence of their mental illness, youth, or other extenuating circumstances been allowed to be presented to a jury.[10]

Texas has an ugly history when it comes to capital punishment—lynching. Texas' long history of vigilante justice and terror influenced the lynching of its citizens, with particular emphasis on lynchings that historically targeted African Americans and Mexican Americans, and it is not far removed from modern-day capital punishment and the Texas culture surrounding it. This history extends as far back as slavery and the Mexican American War. This attitude and cultural perspective still find their way into modern-day criminal justice. Michael Barnes, in his article on lynching in the *Austin American*, chronicled over seven hundred modern-day lynchings that have taken place in the state of Texas. No worse example can be found than the brutal, racially motivated murder of African American James Byrd Jr. in Jasper, Texas, who was dragged behind a pickup truck by three white males for three miles along an asphalt road on June 7, 1998.[11]

Incompetent capital-defense lawyers are also prevalent in Texas. It was Houston attorney John Benn who slept through the capital-defense trial of George McFarland in 1991. When asked about his sleeping in the courtroom, his response regarding the trial was, "It's boring." His client was convicted and eventually executed.

Texas lawyer Jon Wood put up a faulty defense of his client Jesus Romero and concluded the trial with a twenty-word closing argument: "You've got that man's life in your hands. You can take it or not. That's all I have to say." His client, who had credible claims of innocence, was convicted and eventually executed.

Texas lawyer Joe Frank Cannon also had the reputation of continually dozing off. He did so in the trial of Calvin Burdine and Carl Johnson. Each capital defendant appealed their convictions, alleging, among other things, that their sleeping lawyer deprived them of the "effective assistance of counsel," which is a guarantee of the Sixth Amendment right to counsel. Burdine appealed all the way to the United States Supreme Court, where they allowed his conviction to stand. Burdine was eventually able to secure his freedom when a federal judge ordered his release on March 1, 2000, and the prosecution vowed to retry him. He eventually pled guilty and agreed to serve a life sentence. Carl Johnson was executed on September 19, 1995.

Finally, Houston lawyer Jerry Guerinot has the reputation of being the worst lawyer in America. He lost each and every one of his capital cases. Court records show that twenty-one of his clients received the death penalty and ten have been executed, while thirteen of his other clients are serving life sentences. Texas is "Exhibit A" demonstrating the problem with capital punishment in America.

GENDER AS AN ARBITRARY FACTOR

In this country, as a general rule, we do not execute women. We do execute men. We see this factor play out in any number of circumstances. According to our societal mores, we protect the women in our society, even when they commit serious crimes. The exception to this rule is when a woman commits such a heinous crime that we no longer see them as a woman, but rather as something "less than"—a monster, in fact. Take, for example, the case of serial killer Aileen Wuornos, who was convicted and executed in 2002 for the killing of six men. Her crime was such that we no longer viewed her as a "lady," but instead we looked at her as a "monster"—which happened to be the title of a movie made about her life. Aileen was a troubled child, sexually abused as a teen, and kicked out of her home, forcing her to make her living on the street as a prostitute. She suffered from mental illness and was addicted to drugs. She had been treated so badly by so many men that she eventually developed a hatred for the gender and ultimately began murdering male members of her clientele. The fact that she committed these crimes in a Southern state (Florida), was represented by an ineffective trial lawyer, committed crimes that shocked the sensibilities of polite society, and did not have evidence of her abuse or mental illness submitted at trial on her behalf, all served to seal her fate on death row. She was executed in 2002, with her last words recorded as "I'm sailing with the rock, and I'll be back like Independence Day, with Jesus June six. Like the movie, big mother ship and all, I'll be back."

The simple fact is, the death penalty is rarely imposed upon women, and when it is, it is—more often than not—later reduced to a life sentence. In fact, post—*Furman*, 90 percent of women who were sentenced to death had their death sentences reversed. For those women who do receive the death penalty, certain demographics that relate to women ultimately cause them to be executed. Typically, we find that:

- They are poor, uneducated, and from the lowest economic strata.
- Their victims were white, or children, or from another "protected" class (e.g., white males, wealthy, or elderly).
- Most did not have a codefendant.
- The crimes they were convicted of were "shocking" or "unladylike," allowing them to be seen as less-than-wholesome women.

AGE AS AN ARBITRARY FACTOR

We do not execute the elderly. The age of a defendant at the time of the crime has an unjust bearing on the final sentence in a death-eligible trial. Statistically the numbers reveal that anyone over the age of sixty at the time of the commission of a death-eligible crime has virtually no chance of receiving the death penalty, whereas conversely, anyone between the ages of twenty-five and sixty-five is more likely to be executed, with the odds decreasing for defendants over the age of thirty. Juveniles had rarely been executed historically. The Supreme Court put this to a permanent end when they outlawed juvenile executions in *Roper versus Simmons* (2005). While it should be obvious that it is not a sound policy to execute the young, there are some very tenable reasons for not doing so. As a result, legislatures across the country have been very reluctant to execute juveniles, even before *Roper*. These reasons explain why:

- First, it is well-known that juveniles have not matured intellectually as their adult counterparts have, and as a result, their decision-making ability is impaired.
- Next, due to the impulsive nature of juveniles, the death penalty does not function as a deterrent. Most juveniles commit criminal acts without considering the consequences fully, or they lack the knowledge, experience, and understanding to fully appreciate the consequences of their decisions.
- Juveniles are able to be rehabilitated and are young enough to make major life changes.
- No legitimate societal purpose is served by executing juveniles.
- Other nations, particularly those that share our heritage, reject the concept of juvenile executions, as well.

In conclusion, by now it should be obvious that something is fundamentally wrong with a criminal sanction that is so greatly influenced by such mundane, inconsequential factors as age, gender, and geography. There are those who would argue that a certain amount of arbitrariness must be accepted, but safeguards may be infused in the system to prevent tragic consequences. There are others who argue that these very safeguards are what cause unreasonable delays and the exorbitant expense associated with death-penalty administration. While these arguments may be true, we must ask ourselves, are delays and expenses the most critical issue when it comes to legally taking a life? Isn't the preservation of all lives, no matter the background, the goal of our society? If so, then the simple solution is the abolition of capital punishment.

By doing so, we rid ourselves of the delay, the expense, and most importantly, the risk of taking an innocent life.

For this reason alone, the death penalty should be abolished in the United States—but this is not the only reason. There are many more and equally compelling reasons, which we will consider in this book.

NOTES

1. People whose victims are White are more likely to receive the death penalty than those who kill Black persons.

2. Evan J. Mandery, *Capital Punishment in America*, 2nd ed. (Sudbury, MA: Jones and Barlett Learning, 2012), 131.

3. While the Supreme Court did, indeed, abolish capital punishment in *Furman versus Georgia* (1972), it reinstated the legality of capital punishment a mere four years later, with their ruling in *Gregg versus Georgia* (1976).

4. Murderous intent and premeditation are often found in murder statutes as "enhancements" triggering the availability of the death penalty. Being unable to properly define these terms is believed to have led jurors to apply them erroneously, resulting in the imposition of the death penalty when other, less-harsh options, were available.

5. Texas has performed the most executions since 2015; since 1976, there have been 1,352 executions by lethal injection.

6. Whitney Evans, "Virginia Governor Signs Law Abolishing the Death Penalty, A 1st in the South," March 24, 2021, NPR (National Public Radio), https://www.npr.org.

7. Virginia Democratic delegate Jay Jones, speaking on the floor of the Virginia House of Delegates, March 24, 2021, NPR, https:www.npr.org.

8. I have personally represented defendants in the states of Illinois, Indiana, California, Ohio, Minnesota, Georgia, and Wisconsin. Based upon these experiences, it is my opinion that the state of Texas is, by far, the worst state to present a defense and to attempt to protect the rights of individuals who have entered the Texas criminal justice system.

9. See Darah Gregorian, March 18, 2021, www.nbcnews.com.

10. Another key difference in Texas criminal justice is that, unlike in most states, once a person is convicted in a capital case, it is the jury, not the judge, who makes the sentencing determination. The danger to capital defendants in allowing laypersons, regardless of how well-meaning and forthright, to make the ultimate decision without taking into consideration legally significant factors that a trained judge would be required to consider is horrifying. "Why Is Texas #1 Executions?" deathpenaltyinfo.org.

11. In an ironic twist of fate, one of the three men, the purported ringleader, John William King, was himself executed by the state of Texas on June 24, s2019, for this horrendous crime.

Chapter 3

The Financial Cost of Capital Punishment Makes It Illogical to Continue Its Use

Since the reinstatement of modern capital punishment in 1976,[1] there has been an ongoing debate between those who would abolish the sanction and those who want to continue its use. The abolitionists have used numerous and creative arguments to abolish capital punishment, citing its cruelty, its faulty methodology, and a plea for morality. Meanwhile, those who continue to favor its use rely on arguments sounding in retribution, deterrence, and victim's rights.

While neither side seems able to convert the other, a new development has arrived that tends to make both sides of the argument obsolete. Even better, there really is no dispute from either side, in favor of capital punishment, or against capital punishment, about this one particular fact. The simple argument that both sides can agree upon is this—capital punishment trials are much more costly than non-capital trials. It is not even comparably close in cost. The cost of these capital cases is so high, the cases take so long, and they so often fail to end in an execution, that to continue to seek its use makes little, if any economic sense. I would argue that this fact alone is cause enough for the abolition of capital punishment in America. Where appeals to morality, ethics, inequality, and ineffectiveness have failed, appeals to simple dollars and cents is starting to prevail.

THE EXORBITANT COST OF MAINTAINING A SYSTEM OF CAPITAL PUNISHMENT

For many, the issue of capital punishment is a moral one, but for others, the question of fiscal responsibility takes center stage. For those who are concerned about the cost of our criminal justice system, the cost of capital punishment cannot be ignored in the analysis. Capital punishment is an expensive form of punishment, and taxpayers are becoming more aware of the implications of maintaining this costly system.[2] Consider, for example, that defense costs for death-penalty trials in the state of Kansas average almost $400,000 per case, compared to almost $100,000 per case when the death penalty is not sought.[3] A study of Los Angeles, California, county trials showed that the average trial when the death penalty is sought costs $1,898,323, as compared to the average trial in which the death penalty is not sought, which costs $627,322.[4] In fact, a recent study revealed that the state of California has spent over four billion dollars in costs related to capital punishment since 1978. In reaching this conclusion, the study considered the defense attorney's costs, particularly court-appointed ones; the prosecution's costs; courtroom costs; jury-related costs; courtroom work-group costs; pre-trial costs of automatic appeals; and the cost of incarceration on death row.[5]

For years, California has been bearing the costs of maintaining a capital punishment administration while struggling financially, having to cut many essential services while trying to balance the state budget.[6] A 2005 article from the *Los Angeles Times* tallied the annual public costs of maintaining the death penalty in California and found that "it costs $90,000 more per year to house an inmate on death row, where each person has a private cell and an extra guard," than to house a non–death-row inmate.[7] It also found that eleven executions over a twenty-seven-year period cost, on average, $250,000 per execution and that a "capital murder trial costs three times more to try than a noncapital murder trial." Consider these numbers from California: The Office of the State Public Defender, which represents some death-row inmates, has an annual budget of $11.3 million; additionally, the Habeas Corpus Resource Center, which represents inmates and trains death-penalty attorneys, operates on an annual budget of $11 million, and federal public defenders, along with court-appointed attorneys receive $12 million annually. These numbers are crippling to a state budget. With all things considered, from a purely financial perspective, the death penalty exacts a very costly fiscal penalty on taxpayers. In times of drastic budget cuts and reduction of services, notwithstanding other arguments against capital punishment, it would appear that it is fiscally irresponsible to continue to administer such a costly system of punishment.

To shine an illuminating light on this subject, it is important to see why these numbers are so high by examining the associated costs.

COSTS ASSOCIATED WITH CAPITAL PUNISHMENT

Why is capital punishment so expensive? Where are all these taxpayer dollars being spent? These are reasonable questions to ask, and there are simple, reasonable answers to these questions. The fact is, the death penalty is unlike any other form of punishment, and it carries with it specific requirements designed to provide a fair and just determination—first of guilt, then of punishment.

In capital trials, there are two "phases" of the trial. The first phase is the trial phase, during which the capital defendant is tried, with rare exceptions, by a jury. If a capital defendant is found guilty, the next phase of the trial begins, which is called the penalty phase. During this phase, the only determination that ultimately must be made is whether the capital defendant deserves to live, by demonstrating certain redeeming qualities, by submitting facts that mitigate his offense, or by presenting evidence of reduced culpability, or some other major altering factors that support allowing the defendant to avoid execution. Absent such evidence, the capital defendant is sentenced to execution. Attorneys for the capital defendant produce as much evidence as they can find to bolster their argument that their client should have his or her life spared.

As you can see, much must be done and decided before the state can take the life of one of its own citizens. Each step, and each phase, is very costly. Here are typical costs associated with the execution of a capital defendant:

1. Legal costs: More often than not, capital defendants cannot afford to hire their own lawyers once a case has been certified as a death-seeking prosecution. Once court-appointed, the attorney for the defendant is paid for out of taxpayer dollars. Often, two (sometimes more) lawyers are appointed to handle the immense responsibility of the trial. These lawyers are paid on an hourly basis, which is normally capped at a maximum amount. However, there is no prohibition that would prevent defense lawyers from seeking additional payment by petitioning the judge during or after trial. Furthermore, it is not uncommon for these fee petitions to be granted.
2. Pretrial costs: The amount of work that must be done to properly prepare for a capital defense is enormous and can involve several other people, who must also be paid. These include, but are not limited to, expert witnesses, mental health professionals, private investigators, social workers, forensic scientists, and jury consultants.
3. Jury selection: All jury selections are time-consuming, with "standard" *voir dire*, but selecting persons who are willing and qualified to sit

on a capital-punishment jury can be quite a challenge. Not only must potential jurors be free of any real or potential bias toward the defendant, but they must also be willing to impose a verdict of guilt with full knowledge that it will very likely lead to the death of the defendant. Finding the correct mixture of citizens who can pass this test, as well as any other objections by the prosecution or the defense, is exceptionally time-consuming. The accumulation of all this additional time racks up legal expenses as well as juror and court personnel expenses.

4. Incarceration costs: Prison costs are paid by taxpayers; these costs include housing, security, employees, food, clothing, building maintenance, electricity and water, transportation, and expenses related to regular upkeep. Having a death row increases all these costs exponentially. Housing must be tailored for heightened security, extra security personnel must be maintained, specific training for death-row management must be conducted and maintained, a death chamber must be added and maintained, and costs related to the method of execution must be added. All these expenses are in addition to regular prison expenses.
5. Appeals: Every person who is sentenced to be executed is entitled to appeal that sentence. In every death-penalty case, there are mandatory appeal or review requirements before the sentence can be carried out. After the requisite mandatory appeal(s), each defendant is entitled to a series of appeals that can reach all the way to the United States Supreme Court. The appeals process is so long and includes so many options for review that it usually takes decades before a death sentence can be carried out. At each level of review, there are lawyers for the defense and prosecution who must be paid, judges who must be paid, ancillary administrative costs associated with filing each appeal, and the continuation of death-row costs for decades. In the rare but not uncommon event that a new trial is ordered, the process begins all over again, and the costs keep adding up.[8]

A CLOSER LOOK AT THE COST OF CAPITAL PUNISHMENT: THE STATE OF MARYLAND

A comprehensive report by the Justice Initiative looking at the state of Maryland's capital-punishment administration found the following to be true: The average capital-eligible case in which prosecutors do not seek the death penalty costs Maryland taxpayers more than 1.1 million dollars, including $870,000 dollars in prison costs and $250,000 dollars in adjudication costs.[9]

Conversely, a capital-eligible case in which prosecutors unsuccessfully seek the death penalty costs taxpayers 1.8 million dollars, with prison costs of approximately 950,000 dollars and the cost of adjudication on average 850,000 dollars. Not only do these costs apply to the state of Maryland, but they are generally representative across states that still employ capital punishment.[10]

An average capital-eligible case in which the defendant was executed costs approximately three million dollars, with adjudication costs rising to just under 1.7 million dollars. For example, between the years 1978 and 1999, there were fifty-six cases resulting in a death sentence. These cases cost the Maryland taxpayer 107.3 million dollars, with the overall costs associated with capital cases during this time period rising to 186 million dollars.[11]

When assessing the cost of capital punishment, research demonstrates that while appeals are costly, the greatest expenditures occur prior to and during the trial.[12] Even if we were to eliminate all post-conviction proceedings, the death penalty would still be the most expensive sentencing option available in our criminal justice system.[13]

THE FINANCIAL IMPACT OF CAPITAL PUNISHMENT ON THE GENERAL PUBLIC

The diversion of funds from the public finance pool of resources used to maintain a faltering and ineffective system of capital punishment has had a devastating effect on states and municipalities. Unknowingly, in large part, by maintaining a death penalty system, citizens are giving up funds that could be used for:

1. Improving or building public libraries
2. Creating or funding existing mental health–treatment facilities
3. Creating or funding training and rehabilitation centers
4. Increasing and improving education programs
5. Improvement of public schools
6. Funding domestic-violence programs
7. Creating or funding job-creation programs
8. Improving state infrastructure
9. Funding emergency services

It is undeniable just how much these initiatives would improve the lives of taxpayers and benefit communities. The same cannot be said for maintaining a system of capital punishment.

All the sacrifice may, arguably, be worth it if we saw evidence that violent crime was decreasing, or that there were no exonerations from death row due to innocence. Perhaps then we could see some overarching value to maintaining capital punishment. Clearly, however, this is not the case. There can be no value in continuing a system of punishment that fails to accomplish its basic intended purposes.

While we looked at the state of Maryland for sake of comparison, it must be emphasized that the exorbitant costs associated with capital punishment are widespread. Consider, for example the situation in these states as well:

New Jersey

Taxpayers spent 253 million dollars, or approximately eleven million dollars per year over a ten-year period to maintain the capital-punishment option in New Jersey. From the period of 1982 through 2005, the state of New Jersey conducted 197 capital trials and imposed sixty death sentences at an estimated cost of 3.2 million dollars per case. Citing the excessive cost of continuing capital punishment, it was finally abolished in New Jersey on December 17, 2007.[14]

Indiana

Indiana taxpayers spent 741,000 dollars over a sixteen-year period to execute a thirty-year-old man. It would have cost 622,000 dollars over forty-seven years to confine this same person for life. The death penalty continues in Indiana.[15]

Washington

In the state of Washington between the years 1993 and 2003, a death-penalty trial cost an average of 432,000 dollars, where a non–death-penalty trial costs, on average, 153,000 dollars. Capital punishment continues in the state of Washington.[16]

A 2003 legislative audit demonstrated that death-penalty cases cost the taxpayers of Kansas 70 percent more than non–death-seeking trials. The average cost of a death-penalty case is 1.2 million dollars per case. A life-without-parole case could save the taxpayers of Kansas between 400,000 and 500,000 dollars per trial.[17] In Tennessee death trials cost 48 percent more than non–death-seeking trials.[18,19]

Pennsylvania

In 2008, the state of Pennsylvania spent three times more on death-penalty cases than on non–death-seeking cases, or three million dollars per case. Based upon an investigation by the *Reading Eagle*, Pennsylvania taxpayers spent over 350 million dollars on the death penalty during a span of time in which only three executions were carried out. This would have been even more costly but for the three executed defendants' decision to withdraw all further appeals, thus allowing their executions to proceed.

This same newspaper reported that 185 cases on death row at the time of their investigation cost the Pennsylvania taxpayers *conservatively* 351 million dollars. This figure did not include the cost of cases that were overturned, or the cases in which the prosecutor sought the death penalty, but the jury returned a different verdict.[20]

Perhaps John Roman said it best when discussing the results of the investigation: "I think it changes the nature of the debate because what it is saying is, let's not just ask if the death penalty is better than not having a death penalty; it's saying, given the death penalty is far more expensive, is it still worth having?" The answer to that question is pretty clear: No, it is not.

Colorado

On Monday, March 23, 2020, Colorado governor Jared Polis signed a bill authorizing the abolition of capital punishment in the state of Colorado. In doing so, he also commuted the sentences of three persons on death row whom he described as "despicable and guilty individuals." Governor Polis went on to say that the "commutation of [these three is] consistent with the recognition that the death penalty cannot be, and never has been administered equitably in the state of Colorado." Colorado's last execution was in 1997.[21]

California

Perhaps no better example can be made than to look closely at the state of California and the outrageous cost of capital punishment for that state. For years, the state of California has been overwhelmed by the crushing cost of maintaining a capital-punishment system. Consider these facts:

1. Death-row inmates cost 184 million dollars more per year than those sentenced to life in prison without the possibility of parole (LWOP).
2. A death-penalty prosecution costs twenty times more than a LWOP prosecution.

3. The least-expensive death-penalty trial costs 1.1 million dollars more than the most-expensive LWOP case.
4. Jury selection runs three to four weeks longer and costs 200,000 dollars more for a death-penalty case than for a LWOP one.
5. The increased security practices mandated for death-row inmates added over 100,000 dollars to the cost of incarcerating each capital prisoner, for a total of over seventy-one million dollars.[22]

In 2006, California was forced to declare a moratorium until a constitutionally sufficient system of lethal injection could be found. This moratorium was to be temporary, to be lifted once a method was in place that satisfied the current objections to the method of administering the lethal-injection protocol.[23] Recognizing this temporal nature, on March 13, 2019, California governor Gavin Newsom signed an executive order declaring a moratorium, bringing capital punishment in California to a complete stop that can only be overturned by a vote of the citizens of California. The moratorium commuted the sentences of 737 death-row inmates to life without the possibility of parole. It also closed the San Quentin execution chamber, and more importantly, it prevents the state of California from creating a constitutionally legal lethal injection. In doing so, Governor Newsom stated, “Our death penalty system has been—by any measure—a failure.” He went on to say, “It has provided no public safety benefit or value as a deterrent. It has wasted billions of taxpayer dollars. But most of all, the death penalty is absolute, irreversible, and irreparable in the event of human error.”[24]

It does not take much to understand the exasperation of Governor Newsom with his state’s capital punishment administration. A 2006 study conducted by U.S. Court of Appeals judge Arthur L. Alarcon and Loyola Law School professor Paula M. Mitchell found that taxpayers have spent more than four billion dollars on capital punishment since the state reinstated it in 1978—all while, during the same span of time, only thirteen capital defendants were executed. This amounts to 308 million dollars for each capital defendant put to death.

The report also projected that unless substantive and costly changes were made, the cost of maintaining the death penalty would skyrocket to a cost of nine billion dollars by the year 2030.[25] It is estimated that capital trials, enhanced security, and the cost of legal representation will add 184 million dollars to the state’s budget for each year that capital punishment remains a punitive sanction in California.

The bad news gets worse. Michael Millman, the executive director of the California appellate project, said that over three hundred inmates on death row are waiting to be appointed attorneys for their state appeals and federal habeas-corpus petitions. He also noted that in a state with over

250,000 lawyers, there are fewer than one hundred attorneys qualified to handle capital cases. The work is dispiriting and demanding, and the compensation is inadequate.[26]

A DIFFERENT PERSPECTIVE ON THE COST OF CAPITAL PUNISHMENT

Kent Scheidegger, in his article "The Death Penalty and Plea Bargaining,"[27] offers a completely different perspective on the cost of capital punishment. In essence, Scheidegger says, "Wait just a minute. If we remove capital punishment completely, then the maximum sentence that can be imposed is life without the possibility of Parole. It then follows that if this is the maximum sentence, those facing this sentence will want to plea bargain down from there or take their chances at trial. This makes logical sense given that the offender or his attorney already knows that the most they could receive is life, either by plea or by sentence." Scheidegger argues, not unconvincingly, that this mere change will have a significant effect on plea bargaining, and it is likely to increase the number of cases that will go to trial rather than bargaining out. He summarizes this position thusly:

> The widespread assumption that repeal of the death penalty will produce an immediate and dramatic savings in trial costs is not justified on the information currently available. If a state repeals the death penalty but is unwilling to accept a greater number of murderers going free after relatively short sentences, then a greater number of life-sentence cases will probably have to go to trial rather than being resolved by plea. Further research is needed before a reliable estimate of net costs or savings of a state having the death penalty as an available sanction can be made.[28]

The cost of capital punishment, no matter what one's opinion may be regarding its usefulness, cannot be ignored any longer. The cost is too high, and for this singular reason, if for no other, capital punishment must be abolished.

NOTES

1. See *Greg versus Georgia*, 428 U.S. 153 (1976).

2. A Gallup poll in October 2019 revealed that only 56 percent of people still favor capital punishment, while 42 percent are opposed. This is the largest drop in support for capital punishment since its reinstatement in 1976. See "Colorado Abolishes Capital Punishment," NBCNews.com, www.nbcnews.com/news/us-news/colorado-aboljshes-death-penaltyni167231.

3. See Report of the Judicial Council Death Penalty Advisory Committee 1 (Feb. 13, 2014), available at http://deathpenaltyinfo.org/documents/KSCost2014.pdf.

4. See David Erickson, "Death Penalty Focus of Cal., Capital Punishment at What Price: An Analysis of the Cost Issue in a Strategy to Abolish the Death Penalty," 25 (Spring 1993). It should also be noted that most of the costs of death-penalty cases result from legal fees.

5. See Judge Arthur L. Alarcon and Paula M. Mitchell, "Executing the Will of the Voters?: A Roadmap to Mend or End the California's Legislature's Multi-Billion-Dollar Death Penalty Debacle," 44 LOY. L.A. L. REV.S41 (2011).

6. See Dan Walters, "California Budget Is Balanced? Not by a Long Shot," *Sacramento Bee* (Mar. 30, 2014), http://www.sacbee.com/news/politics-government/dam-walters/artice2594117.html.

7. Financial Facts about the Death Penalty in America. California: Report of the California Commission on the Fair Administration of Justice (June 30, 2008). www.ccfaj.org.

8. Rone Tempest, "Death Row Often Means a Long Life," *L.A. Times* (Mar. 6, 2005), http://articles.latimes.com/2005/mar/06/local/me-deathpen6.

9. See Death Penalty Information Center, citing Maryland Commission on Capital Punishment, https://deathpenaltyinfo.org/stories/Maryland-commission-on-capital-punishment, retrieved March 6, 2020.

10. Ibid.

11. Ibid.

12. See Recent Cost Studies, Amnesty International, https://www.amnestyusa.org/issues/death-penaltv/deathpenalty-facts/death-penalty-cost/, retrieved March 24, 2020.

13. Ibid.

14. "The High Cost of New Jersey's Death Penalty," https://www.njadp.org/gadabout&what=cost, retrieved March 25, 2020.

15. "Indiana Editorial Calls for End to 'Costly Death Penalty,'" 2005.

16. Bohm, *Death Quest*, 213.

17. Ibid.

18. See Death Penalty Information Center (DPIC), https://deathpenaltyinfo.org/news/pennslyvania-death-penaltycosts, retrieved March 22, 2020; see also Bohm, *Death Quest*, 212.

19. Ibid.

20. See Death Penalty Information Center (DPIC), https://deathpenaltyinfo.org/news/pennslyvania-death-penaltycosts-estimted-at-350-million, retrieved March 23, 2020.

21. See NBCNews.com, www.nbcnews.com/news/us-news/colorado-abolishes-death-penalty-n1167231.

22. See "Death Penalty Costs California $184 Million a Year, Study Says," *Los Angeles Times*, June 2, 2011.

23. See *People versus Ernest Dewayne Jones* (2006), ruling by the Honorable Carmac Carney, Ninth Circuit Court of Appeals.

24. "Governor Gavin Newsom Suspends Death Penalty in California," *National Public Radio*, https://www.npr.org/2019/03/12/702873258/gov-gavin-newsom-suspends-death-penalty-in-california.

25. Ibid.

26. "California Governor Declares Death Penalty Moratorium," March 14, 2019, https://www.death penalty.procon.org/california-governor-declares-d death-penalty-moratorium.

27. Kent Scheidegger, "The Death Penalty and Plea Bargaining to Life Sentences," Criminal Justice Foundation (2009), cited in *Capital Punishment in America*, 2nd ed., Evan J. Mandery, ed. (Burlington, MA: Jones and Bartlett Press, 2012), 101–04.

28. Ibid., 104.

Chapter 4

Capital Punishment Runs Counter to the United States Constitution by Violating the Eighth Amendment's Prohibition against "Cruel and Unusual Punishment"

> *"Excessive bail shall not be required, nor excessive fines imposed, nor shall cruel and unusual punishment be inflicted."*
>
> —The Eighth Amendment to the United States Constitution

One of the most compelling and unavoidable aspects of the death penalty is that it has the potential to touch upon so many aspects of the administration of criminal justice—crime investigation, forensics, evidence, interrogations, prosecutorial decision-making, public-defender systems, judicial education, post-conviction appeals processes, and more. While no system is perfect, when it comes to taking the life of a human being, we should always strive for perfection. In doing so, whether an individual is in favor of capital punishment or is opposed to its continued use, certain problems in the administration of the death penalty should concern us all.

If we are going to give capital punishment serious scrutiny, we will eventually have to face the question of determining the constitutional meaning of the Eight Amendment's prohibition against "cruel and unusual" punishment. We will have to decide if the manner in which we execute offenders equates to the infliction of prohibited amounts of pain during this form of punishment. We must decide what is the acceptable amount of pain that accompanies an execution or if any amount is acceptable at all. We must decide whether an excessive amount of pain during an execution is what the Constitution was referring to when it prohibited cruel and unusual punishment. If so, then we must come to an acceptable understanding of just what is "cruel and unusual" punishment.

What we do know is that the Eighth Amendment to the United States Constitution clearly prohibits the infliction of cruel and unusual punishment. We also know that practically every state constitution has some version of this prohibition as well. Further, it seems to be agreed upon that at the very minimum, cruel and unusual punishment means "excessive" punishment.

But what, then, constitutes excessive punishment? We could argue that Florida's extremely long period on which the condemned must wait on death row—an average of fourteen years—is excessive. We could also argue that the fact that, nationally, more than half the inmates currently sentenced to death have been on death row for eighteen years or more is also excessive. We certainly can argue that the current methods of execution, with their well-documented flaws, are excessive, and we could conclude, for the sake of argument, that this is thereby cruel and unusual. But does this violate the Eight Amendment? I submit that it does.

The fact is, if we examine the most common methods employed to execute the condemned, we find that practically all experts are opposed to the electric chair as a method of execution, and they are equally opposed to the use of lethal gas (the gas chamber) due to the very high probability of an error, or an incomplete execution. Further, while lethal injection is not as vehemently opposed, it is nonetheless opposed as being inconsistent, insufficient, and just slightly more tenable than the electric chair or gas chamber in terms of efficiency without causing undue harm or pain. Professor Deborah Denno, arguably the leading scholarly voice in this area, offers the idea that the risk of a botched execution—which is substantial, she argues—and the pain associated with any form of execution, is a conclusive argument against all three methods of execution.[1]

Conversely, renowned professor and Harvard Law graduate Evan Mandery suggests this is the wrong analysis to employ with respect to the issue of pain and its excessiveness. He argues, "The relevant inquiry is not whether the amount of pain experienced by the executed inmate is substantial or even overwhelming." He continues, "The relevant question is whether it is excessive in comparison to what the inmate would otherwise suffer, or for the want of a crystal ball, what he could expect to suffer in the average case."[2] I respectfully disagree with this view and argue that the inquiry ends once we determine it is excessive. We need not compare it further.

Regardless, it is ultimately not up to lawyers and scholars to determine what constitutes cruel and unusual punishment. This determination can only be made by the United States Supreme Court. For almost 120 years, the Supreme Court dodged the issue of defining "cruel and unusual" by adhering to a fixed interpretation that basically stated whatever was used at the time of the adoption of the Eighth Amendment, in 1791, was, by definition, *not* "cruel" nor "unusual." Over these 120 years, the court has attempted to point out the types of punishments that would be prohibited, such as those that involved live impalement, beheading, and quartering (*Wilkerson versus Utah*, 1878). The court also decided that any punishment that involved torture was prohibited by the Eighth Amendment, such as crucifixion, burning at the stake, or breaking on the wheel (*In re Kemmler*, 1890).[3]

By 1910, in *Weems versus the United States*, the Court was ready to try to classify further what was, or was not, cruel and unusual punishment. It held in a non–death-penalty case that the meaning of the Eighth Amendment is not restricted to the intent of the Framers; it bars punishments that are excessive and "that which is excessive is not fixed in time but changes with evolving social conditions."[4] Fifty years later, the Court went even further to clarify what is, and is not, cruel and unusual punishment in another non–death-penalty case, this time in *Trope versus Dulles* (1958). In this case, Mr. Trope was convicted and punished for desertion during World War II and received, among other punishments, the punishment of being stripped of his United States citizenship. Upon review the Supreme Court ruled this was a step too far and called it an "affront to basic human dignity." It went further to say that "the dignity of man" was the basic concept underlying the Eighth Amendment and ruled that this punishment exceeded the limits of civilized standards.[5]

Simply put, the "cruel and unusual punishment" clause measures a particular punishment against inhumane treatment. It prevents the government from imposing a penalty that is either barbaric or far too severe for the crime committed. Historically, the meaning applied to "cruel and unusual" was "whatever means" of execution that was allowed at the time of adoption of the Bill of Rights (1791) would be allowed to continue. This definition lasted for over 120 years with only the most barbaric forms of punishment prohibited.

As noted, the *Weems* case created a new definition of what is "cruel and unusual" and specifically stated that this is not bound by the Framers' intent but is that which "evolves with changing social conditions." When the Supreme Court used the phrase "evolving standards of decency," the floodgates were opened to new interpretations and new legal standards, which continue to be presented to this day. Challenges have ensued regarding such issues as sanitation, heating and cooling, pest control, toilets and plumbing, lighting, laundry, mental-health issues, exercise, execution of the elderly, length of stay on death row, and virtually any issue that smart lawyers can conceive to attach to the Eighth Amendment's prohibition against "cruel and unusual punishment." It is my expectation that the Court will continue to struggle with a working definition of what constitutes "cruel and unusual" as long as the standard exists.

While the Supreme Court has tackled this definitional issue in a number of cases, none has been more crucial than their inquiry in 1972. The Supreme Court had the question posed squarely before them: Does the Eighth Amendment prohibit the death penalty? Is capital punishment "cruel and unusual punishment"? To answer these questions, the Supreme Court agreed to hear four test cases. They were:

1. *Aikens versus California*, 406 U.S. 813 (1972);
2. *Branch versus Texas*, 537 U.S. 1198 (1972);
3. *Jackson versus Georgia*, 92 S. Ct. 2726 (1972); and
4. *Furman versus Georgia*, 408 U.S. 238 (1972).

These cases have commonly been known as *Furman versus Georgia* (1972). In their reasoning, the Court announced the limitations of their inquiry into "cruel and unusual" by stating, "There are, then, four principles by which we may determine whether a particular punishment is 'cruel and unusual.'" They then listed the four principles:

- The essential predicate is that a punishment must not by its severity be degrading to human dignity, especially torture.
- It must not be a severe punishment that is obviously inflicted in wholly arbitrary fashion.
- It must not be a severe punishment that is clearly and totally rejected throughout society.
- It must not be a severe punishment that is patently unnecessary.

To make their determination, they had to apply these principles to the facts of the case they were reviewing. The facts of the *Furman* case were these: Mr. Furman committed murder in a failed robbery attempt. His victim, William Micke, was a Coast Guard officer and a father of four and a stepfather of six. Furman's lawyer was paid $150 by the state of Georgia to defend him. The request for a private investigator was denied. The entire trial lasted one single day. Mr. Furman was diagnosed as mentally deficient, with an IQ of sixty-five. Notwithstanding, the jury imposed the death sentence. The sentence was appealed.

On appeal, Furman's lawyer made these arguments:

1. Giving a jury the option to impose life or death was "arbitrary and capricious," in violation of the Constitution.
2. Executing a mentally handicapped man violates the basic elements of criminal responsibility by eliminating the mental state requirement.

3. The methods of execution are "cruel and unusual" in violation of the Eighth Amendment.

What the Supreme Court was most concerned with in *Furman* was not simply whether executing a person was, by definition, "cruel and unusual," but their inquiry extended to whether the method of execution was a significant factor in determining whether the punishment, in and of itself, was "cruel and unusual." After completing their review and applying the facts to the four principles they set forth, for the very first time, the Supreme Court, in a 5–4 decision, determined that the death penalty specifically violated the prohibition against cruel and unusual punishment.

It is important to note that at the time of the *Furman* decision in 1972, the common and preferred method of execution was lethal injection. Lethal injection was chosen as the preferred method for the very reason that it, at least on its surface, appeared to be more humane. Typically, this method employed a three-drug protocol. The first drug introduced into the victim's body in this process is typically midazolam, for sedation purposes. Next is the introduction of pancuronium bromide (Pavulon), which is used to cause muscle paralysis and respiratory arrest. The final protocol is potassium chloride, used to stop the heart from beating. Lethal injection came to be preferred after horrific experiences with hanging and electrocution as methods of execution. It was believed that this three-drug protocol would prevent such horrific experiences. I submit that it has not.

It is important to remember that the problem of methodology has been with us since capital punishment was introduced. In this country alone, we have employed beheading, pressing to death, drawing and quartering, breaking on the wheel, drowning, burning at the stake, firing squad, hanging, electrocution, lethal gas, and now lethal injection. All these methods were designed to execute with certainty, and as humanely and painlessly as possible. To that end, lethal injection was seen as the cure for Eighth Amendment challenges in that it was seen as painless and capable of being carried out in such a manner as to respect the dignity of life. Supporters of this method opined, "How could there be a more pain-free method of execution?" The assumption here is that after the introduction of the drugs sequentially, the condemned is executed during a peaceful sleep.

This opinion, however, is an oversimplification. It does not consider the possibility of problems with the drugs being administered in improper doses and the painful effect this may have on the unconscious condemned. This opinion does not consider how the effect that the skill and training, or lack thereof, of the person administering the injections may have an excessively painful effect on the condemned, nor does it consider how the improperly administered injection of lethal drugs could cause excessive pain and prolonged agony before the condemned expires. Clearly, lethal injection is not the complete answer when trying to avoid that which is cruel and unusual during executions.

Setting aside, for the moment, the question of whether lethal injection is painless or more humane, let's consider the actual process of carrying out a death sentence. What we find is that systemically, cruelty is woven into the process.

Before a defendant can be executed, that defendant must be given the opportunity for a judicial determination of guilt and punishment. It is the prosecutor who announces early in the prosecution that she will be seeking the death penalty. From this point forward, the defendant is aware that it is the intention of the State to take his life. The possibility of this eventuality hangs over every hearing, every motion, literally every effort that is made for what usually turns out to be decades.

The trial itself underscores this eventuality. Procedurally, after a finding of guilt in a death-eligible trial, there is a second proceeding, referred to as the penalty phase, in which the defendant is forced to attempt to prove that his life is worth saving. To do so, his life is examined by any number of experts or laypersons, friends, teachers, siblings, social workers, parents, and any other person imaginable who is in a position to argue that this person's life should not be extinguished. The inherent immorality of forcing a person to prove what is freely given at birth—i.e., the right to exist—is inescapable. Yet the torture continues.

After a finding of guilt, and a determination that there are not enough redeeming qualities present to preserve the defendant's life, he is sent to a maximum-security prison and housed in a special unit commonly referred to as death row, where he will be held in solitary confinement with limited space, virtually no activities, and no access to programs or self-development opportunities.

The condemned is forced to sit and wait, for what often is decades, for his death sentence to be carried out. During this interminable wait, the death penalty victim is teased with the hope of the appellate process, which, for the rare few, may overturn his conviction, award a new trial, stay his execution, or provide some other form of permanent or temporary relief. This roller coaster of execution date set—to execution date delayed—to execution date reset continues to play out over a period of years until all appellate options have expired and the sentence may be carried out. There have been many occasions when the death sentence has come within days, hours, or even minutes of being carried out, before being judicially halted by the appellate process. One can only imagine what this must do to the psyche of the death-penalty victim under the stress of extreme isolation. One of the best descriptions of what this was like was provided by Ron Williamson, the subject of legendary author of legal thrillers John Grisham, in his work *The Innocent Man: Murder and Injustice in a Small Town.* In this book, Ron Williamson recounts the horrors of being on death row. Based upon his description, and the descriptions of many others similarly situated, there is absolutely nothing humane about the process.

If we simply pause for a moment and examine what we have been doing with regard to the administration of capital punishment, we will see a failed death penalty system. We would see that after all this time, we continue to contort ourselves legally, trying to find a method of execution that does not shock the senses, is consistent with our perceptions of civility, and does not cause undue pain or extensive harm beyond the actual cause of death itself, while trying to address the numerous and legitimate challenges to the application of cruel and unusual punishment prohibited by the Eighth Amendment. In my view, we have failed at every turn, and I would further submit that this failure will persist. We cannot legally kill another human being without violating the Eighth Amendment's prohibition against anything that constitutes cruel and unusual punishment. As a result of this inability and our history of futility, we should abolish capital punishment as a punitive sanction.

NOTES

1. See Evan J. Mandery, *Capital Punishment in America: A Balanced Examination*, p. 492 (Sudbury, MA: Jones & Bartlett Learning, LLC, 2012).
2. Ibid.
3. See, for further explanation, Robert M. Bohm, *Death Quest III* (2007), p. 146.
4. See *Weems versus United States*, 217 U.S. 349 (1910).
5. See *Trop versus Dulles*, 356 U.S. 86 (1958).

Chapter 5

Lethal Injection: An Inherently Flawed Method of Execution

THERE IS NO HUMANE WAY TO EXECUTE A PERSON: SOME ARE JUST LESS HORRIFIC THAN OTHERS

We previously discussed some of the problems with capital punishment. Some of these problems are at the administrative level (involving financial costs); others force us to ask who should be executed (involving arbitrariness); and we even examined our history with this sanction starting in the 1600s and leading up to modern times. However, none of these issues attempts to get at the heart of the problem, which we will examine now. The question is, Just *how* should we take the life of another human being? It is not so difficult to exclaim that a person who commits a certain crime should be put to death. It is not that personal to write legislation calling for the execution of particular offenders, but when it comes to the actual killing, this makes things much more difficult.

Let me state clearly from the outset, there is no humane way to execute another human being. No matter how it is done, when death is the final outcome, something horrible has happened to a human body. We spend our lives trying to make life safer, trying to create advances in medicine to prolong life, and coming up with rules and procedures designed to save lives. We do this almost instinctively, because there is an innate recognition of the value of life—any life. The taking of a life is in direct opposition to all of this. The simple proposition of executing someone raises a whole host of difficult and ethically challenging questions, such as: What is the proper method of executing someone? Where should our priorities lie? Should we consider the cost? Should we consider the efficiency of the method chosen? Should the pain caused to the defendant be a consideration? Is the length of time it takes to complete the execution a proper consideration? Should we consider the effect that taking a life has on the actual executioner? Should the damage caused to the body be a factor of consideration? All these questions, and many others, our criminal justice system has grappled with at one time or another, and it has come up with no real satisfactory answer. The Supreme Court has waffled on these issues as well, interpreting and reinterpreting over the course of time. What emerges is the clearly obvious answer that there is no "good" way to kill another human being. And while the current and preferred method of execution is lethal injection, this, too, is an inherently flawed method.

It is important that we look at how we settled upon lethal injection as opposed to some of the other, absolutely barbaric methods employed in the past. I am often amazed at how cruel human beings can be to other human beings when given the power to do so, and the method of execution is no exception. Consider that throughout the course of world history, the death penalty has been carried out by stoning to death, flaying and impaling, boiling in oil, feeding to the lions, crucifixion, pulling asunder, burying alive, and sawing in half.[1] Thankfully, none of these methods were ever legally used in the United States, but we can take very little comfort in this fact when we consider that beheading, pressing to death, drawing and quartering, breaking on the wheel, drowning, and burning at the stake[2] all, at one time or another, were legal methods of execution in the United States.

We have evolved as a nation, and our methods of killing have also evolved to more modern methods that are, some would argue, less gruesome, more humane, and less apt to violate the Eighth Amendment's prohibition against cruel and unusual punishment. The four modern methods of execution are electrocution, the lethal gas chamber, hanging, and lethal injection, with death by firing squad also worthy of mention since it is still an option in certain jurisdictions under certain circumstances.[3]

DEATH BY ASPHYXIATION (HANGING)

Hanging was one of the first lawful[4] and widely used methods in the United States. One look at any classic Western movie portrayal of the "Old West" will quickly reveal the prevalence of this method of execution. There are three states that still allow hanging as an alternative when lethal injection is unavailable; they are Delaware, New Hampshire, and the state of Washington.[5] It is believed that more Americans have been executed by hanging than by any other method of execution.[6] The slow and agonizing death caused by hanging was meant to deter the public and to publicly humiliate the offender. This method of execution, however, was not without its problems;

there were many botched hangings in which the defendant did not die for an extraordinary length of time, instances when the weight of the victim and the length of the rope were miscalculated causing either the rope to break or the stanchion employed to snap. There were also instances when the "drop" was so long and the weight of the victim so heavy that when the rope was sturdy enough not to break, it literally would cause the head to break free of the body, resulting in the body and head to land in different locations.[7] The fact is, there were numerous botched hangings for one reason or another. Between 1622 and 2022, at least 170 botched hangings occurred in the United States.[8]

DEATH BY ELECTROCUTION

The electric chair was introduced in 1890 as a new way of executing individuals, touted to be more humane and less gruesome. If only this were true.

Death by electrocution, commonly referred to as the "electric chair," started out as a gimmick, as part of a corporate battle between two companies: Westinghouse and Edison. The Edison Company, created by the great scientist Thomas Edison, was in a battle with Westinghouse to determine which company would ultimately provide electricity to the cities of America.[9] In essence, the choice was between Westinghouse's alternating current (AC) method or Edison's direct current (DC) method of producing electricity. Westinghouse's AC method was cheaper and had a larger range of effectiveness. In an effort to expose the dangers of the AC method of current production, the Edison Company staged public demonstrations in which animals were electrocuted using the AC method to show just how dangerous the Westinghouse product was.

Dr. Alfred P. Southwick, a dentist from New York, took note of these demonstrations and tried similar experiments of his own. He had also witnessed a man electrocuted by touching an electric generator.[10] The governor of New York, unhappy with hanging as the method of execution for his state, appointed Dr. Southwick to a three-person commission to determine "the most humane and practical method of execution known to science." Southwick, with the aid of Thomas Edison, was able to persuade the other commission members to endorse electrocution as the preferred method of execution, replacing hanging in the state of New York.[11]

The first person to be executed by electrocution was William Kemmler, on August 6, 1890. This method of execution was flawed from the start. Kemmler did not die instantaneously; a second jolt was required four and a half minutes after the first jolt of electricity. After the second jolt of electricity, eyewitnesses stated that Kemmler's hair and flesh burned, blood was on his face, and his body emitted a horrible stench.[12] Despite this botched first attempt at electrocution, and numerous accounts of other botched attempts with horrible, painful, and gruesome results, electrocution became the method used by the majority of death penalty states between 1930 and 1972. Here are a few newspaper accounts describing botched electrocutions:

> "The State's first try at executing Alpha Otis Stephens in the electric chair failed today, and he struggled to breathe for eight minutes before a second jolt carried out his death sentence."[13]

> "Five jolts of electricity instead of the prescribed two were needed . . . to execute William Vandiver. . . . A prison Doctor said that Vandiver was still breathing after the first round of 2,300 volts and second of 500 volts. Three more blasts of current were applied before he was pronounced dead 17 minutes later."[14] [Michigan City, Indiana]

> "When the first jolt of 2,000-volt electricity hit [Jesse] Tafero, the sponge in the headpiece gave off a combustible gas, which shot smoke and flames from the top of the leather hood hiding Tafero's face. The flames, described as 3 inches to a foot long, horrified witnesses. Tafero's attorney described the flawed execution as torture."[15]

Clearly, electrocution did not turn out to be the panacea that proponents of its use had hoped for. It should be noted that the Supreme Court dodged the question of whether the use of electrocution violated the Eighth Amendment's prohibition against cruel and unusual punishment. In a pattern that has been repeated to this day, the Supreme Court failed to tackle the problem when the issue was first presented in the William Kemmler case.[16] Kemmler's lawyer argued that electrocution was cruel and unusual in an attempt to halt his execution; however, the Court refused to address this claim, arguing that the Eighth Amendment did not apply to the states. By taking such an extremely restrictive view of the Eighth Amendment, the Court did not have to consider the claims made by the New York legislature that electrocution produced an "instantaneous" and "painless" death. It is shameful that our Supreme Court has far too often chosen to avoid addressing the issues of capital punishment by dancing around facts that clearly reveal a system fraught with cruel and unusual punishment.

DEATH BY LETHAL GAS

Since hanging was no longer the preferred method, and electrocution turned out to be less than humane, the search for the next best way to kill a convicted criminal did not take long to come up with a new method: lethal gas.

In 1921, the Nevada legislature passed a Humane Death Bill, whereby, among other things, hanging was replaced by lethal gas, which first gained public attention after its use in World War I. In a twist of irony, the governor of Nevada reluctantly signed this new legislation believing it would not survive as it was clearly a cruel and unusual way to execute a person.[17]

In a twist of fate that could not have been written if planned, the first execution by lethal gas was a horrendous failure, while also, admittedly, a success. Gee Jon, a Chinese crime association member who was convicted in a gangland murder, has the dubious distinction of being the first to have been executed by lethal gas. The original plan was to execute Jon by administering lethal gas to him in his cell while he slept without notice. It wasn't long before administrators realized the glaring flaw in their plan. While the lethal gas would most assuredly kill Gee Jon, there was no way to contain its reach of contamination, and the gas would likely also kill other unintended inmates and potentially prison personnel. To solve the problem, a chamber was quickly built, and on February 8, 1924, Jon became the first person to be lawfully executed by lethal cyanide gas. Several other states were quick to follow Nevada's lead and adopted lethal gas as the form to be used in executions.[18]

As lethal gas became more popular as the "latest" method of execution, certain problems became apparent. The use of lethal gas faced the normal Eighth Amendment challenges, and the Supreme Court continued to avoid, ignore, or insist that death by lethal gas did not violate the prohibition against cruel and unusual punishment.[19] But a more practical problem caused the continued use of lethal gas to come into question, and that problem was cost. It should not come as a surprise that the maintenance of gas chambers could be expensive. They needed to be airtight, checked regularly, and cleared for use so as not to become a hazard for unintended victims. Add to these issues the fact that the chambers did not receive regular use, given the amount of time between executions at some facilities, and the excitement for adopting this method of execution began to wane. Certainly there had to be a better, more humane, less expensive method of executing those sentenced to die.

DEATH BY LETHAL INJECTION

The search for an elusive humane and painless—or at least acceptably painful—method of execution out of necessity continued beyond lethal gas. The solution that the search landed upon was lethal injection. On May 11, 1977, Oklahoma became the first state to authorize lethal injection as its official method of execution. Other states quickly followed, and lethal injection in very short order became the preferred method of execution throughout the death penalty states and the federal government. The process is pretty straightforward in that the inmate is injected with chemicals that will cause his death. It began typically with a three-drug protocol, to include:

1. The induction intravenously of sodium thiopental or sodium pentothal, a barbiturate designed, in this instance, to quickly induce sleep or loss of consciousness.
2. The immediately following injection of pancuronium bromide, a muscle relaxant when, if given properly, stops the ability of the inmate to breathe through paralysis.
3. A final injection of potassium chloride, which induces cardiac arrest and permanently stops the heart from beating.

This method of execution was touted to be more humane, in that purportedly the inmate simply went into a painless sleep before death. It was supposed to be more cost-efficient,[20]as the amount of drugs used was miniscule in comparison to lethal gas and electrocution. Finally, as the argument goes, the end result was less gruesome and more reliable than the previous methods of hanging, electrocution, and lethal gas. Again, if only this were true.

It did not take long before questions arose about this "new" method of execution, and doubts were raised about just how "pain-free" this form of execution truly was. What if the drugs were not administered properly? What if the dosages were not adequate? How much pain would the condemned have to endure if, once paralyzed, the potassium chloride was not administered in a lethal dose? Here is the problem with lethal injection: If the anesthesia is improperly administered or the offender is given an improper dose—too much or too little—the offender may appear to be unconscious when, in fact, they are completely aware of what is happening to them but unable to indicate this due to the induced paralysis. Under these conditions, the offender may feel the painful effects of the paralytic along with the subsequent burning of the potassium chloride.[21] Anesthesiologists spend years in medical school and countless hours in training learning just how to administer drugs and medicine properly based upon any number of factors, including age, weight, medical history, gender, height, and symptomology, yet there are times when even these trained professionals do not get it right, albeit under the most-optimum medical conditions in fully staffed and equipped medical facilities.

Far from being trained properly, most prison personnel conducting executions have had very little medical training. Some jurisdictions have used lethal-injection machines, while others employ executioners selected by the governor of that jurisdiction. It should come as no surprise that these attempts at lethal injection often go awry. Consider the account of the 1988 execution of Raymond Landry in Texas:

> Prison officials began administering the lethal dosage [to Landry] at 12:21 a.m. Landry was not pronounced dead until 24 minutes later. In between, a tube attached to a needle inside his right arm began leaking, sending the lethal mixture shooting across the death chamber toward witnesses. "There was something of a delay in the execution because of what officials called a 'blowout'. . . . The syringe came out of the vein and the warden ordered the execution team to reinsert the catheter into the vein." The leak occurred two minutes after the injections began.[22]

Beyond these practical questions, ethical questions have also been raised about who is involved in what is, ultimately, a medical procedure, and what is the required training and certification, if any. Several medical associations that develop the guidelines used by medical personnel have weighed in on this issue by clearly forbidding medical personnel from participating in lethal injections; these organizations include the American Medical Association, the American College of Physicians, the American Society of Anesthesiologists, and the American Nurses Association. Participation in lethal injection by any member of these organizations could result in loss of membership status. The American Medical Association in 1980 passed a resolution urging all doctors not to participate in executions beyond pronouncing an inmate dead. To participate in any other way would be to violate the Hippocratic Oath and international medical principles and would represent "a corruption and exploitation of the healing profession's role in society."[23]

The American Board of Anesthesiology has gone even further by creating severe sanctions for any participant in lethal injection. As of 2010, the ABA announced that if an anesthesiologist participates in an execution, he will lose his board certification. This could mean an end to that medical professional's medical career. As a result, correction officials are left to appoint execution teams—phlebotomists, medical assistants, EMTs, and military medics—instead of properly trained professionals. Without a physician present to monitor the process or advise what to do when problems arise, there will be many more botched lethal injections, causing untold pain and suffering—or, in other terms, "cruel and unusual punishment."

It should not come as a surprise to note that the legality of lethal injection found its way to the United States Supreme Court. In 2008, the Court took it upon themselves to consider whether the three-drug protocol was capable of passing Eighth Amendment scrutiny. In *Baze and Bowling versus Rees*,[24] the Supreme Court considered the claims by two gentlemen on Kentucky's death row alleging that the three-drug protocol, the same protocol used by most death-penalty states, had the potential to result in "unnecessary pain and suffering." Kentucky used sodium thiopental, pancuronium bromide, and potassium chloride as its three death drugs. This case, heralded by most death-penalty abolitionists, was seen as the best chance of eradicating capital punishment since Thurgood Marshall's 1972 landmark decision in *Furman versus Georgia*, which briefly declared capital punishment unconstitutional,[25] squarely placing the onus on violations of the Eighth Amendment's prohibition against cruel and unusual punishment.

With the *Baze* decision, once more the Supreme Court found a way to justify the untenable. In a 7–2 vote, the Court upheld the constitutionality of lethal injection, ruling that the administration of the three-drug protocol does not "create a substantial risk of wanton and unnecessary infliction of pain, torture, or lingering death."[26] They thereby allowed death-penalty states to continue using lethal injection. The Supreme Court purposefully ignored the fact that there had already been numerous botched attempts at death by lethal injection, with harrowing results certain to violate the prohibition against cruel and unusual punishment.[27]

Ohio, anticipating additional challenges, was the first state to adopt a one-drug protocol, consisting of one continuous flow of the three drug chemicals until the offender is pronounced dead. Other states soon followed Ohio's example. What they could not have anticipated was the practical problem facing lethal injection that would follow: the lack of drugs.

As if these problems were not enough, the added problem of who would manufacture and supply the lethal drugs to the prisons for the execution of inmates has become a very large hurdle in the practical administration of the death penalty. Generally speaking, few companies want to be known as the company that provides the chemicals that makes lethal injections possible. This is not the kind of thing that CEOs often brag about at annual shareholder meetings. However, aside from the less-than-complimentary optics, some international companies from countries that no longer impose the death penalty strictly prohibit the use of their products for the purposes of lethal injections. The concern over access to drugs for lethal injection is centered primarily on sodium thiopental, or the first drug in the three-drug protocol. In 2009, the American maker of sodium thiopental, Hospira, ceased production after it became increasingly more difficult to obtain the key ingredients from their manufacturers. Hospira considered producing the drug from one of their Italian plants, but the Italian government required them to ensure that the drugs would not be used for lethal injection in the United States. In 2010, the British government, another ardent opponent of capital punishment, banned all exports of sodium thiopental to the United States after learning it was being sought for use in the administration of lethal injections.[28] As a result of the diminishing supply of sodium thiopental, prison officials began purchasing the drugs from other countries, but in 2011, the U.S. Drug Enforcement Agency (DEA) confiscated supplies of sodium thiopental from states that purchased it from international sources because they failed to meet U.S. standards of importation.

The inability to obtain sodium thiopental resulted in death-penalty states needing to find a substitute. They quickly settled upon pentobarbital. It was not long before there were problems with this drug as well. Unlike sodium thiopental, pentobarbital is not commonly used on humans. It is best known for its use by veterinarians to anesthetize or euthanize animals. The exact same concerns exist with the use of pentobarbital as with sodium thiopental in terms of efficacy and availability. Missouri took things a step further and attempted to obtain propofol (the same drug that led to Michael Jackson's untimely demise), but the European manufacturers refused to sell it to corrections facilities, leaving correction administrations across the country scrambling to locate drugs to be used for executions.

The irony in all this cannot be escaped. American correctional facilities are searching the globe to buy black market drugs because legal suppliers will not sell to them due to their intended use. Our system of death-penalty administration has been reduced to a ghastly parody of the drug dealer–drug addict relationship in search of a reliable supplier.

I had the pleasure of serving on a panel with leading scholars debating the issue of the continued use of capital punishment at the University of Miami School of Law. Foremost among them was law professor Debra Denno, the Arthur A. McGivney Professor of Law at Fordham University School of Law. Professor Denno is unquestionably one of the world's leading scholars on the ills of capital punishment, and a staunch advocate for its permanent abolition. Professor Denno argues that if the Supreme Court was willing to hear Eighth Amendment challenges to all current execution methods, to consider available evidence demonstrating the cruelty of these methods, and apply the evolving-standards-of-decency criteria, it would be forced to conclude that all current methods of executions are unconstitutional. Denno further believes that if the Court was to follow such a course, it would have to declare the death penalty itself unconstitutional because no method of punishment could meet the required standards.[29]

What should be clearly obvious by now is that there really is no humane method to kill another human being. Our criminal justice system should not be in the business of killing others. Some of our closest allies around the world, with histories that span hundreds of years longer than the existence of the United States, have all arrived at the same conclusion—there is no humane method of execution. (We are literally sandwiched between two countries—Canada and Mexico—that have no death penalty and will not extradite an offender headed for capital punishment.) If we accept this reality, the question then shifts from what is the most pain-free method of execution, to the real underlying question: If we cannot execute humanely, and we consider ourselves to be a humane society, then we cannot be both humane and sanction a governmental inhumane act. If for no other reason than this, the death penalty must be abolished. However, there are many more reasons than this.

NOTES

1. Bohm, 145; see also Virginia Leigh Hatch and Anthony Walsh, *Capital Punishment: Theory and Practice of the Ultimate Penalty* (Oxford: Oxford University Press, 2016).

2. This particularly heinous method of execution was reserved for special categories of crimes, an extra cruelty to theoretically maximize the deterrent effect, such as the murdering of an owner by a slave or the murder of a husband by his wife. See Bohm, *Death Quest III*, 145.

3. Methods of execution, Death Penalty Information Center, www.deathpenaltyinfo .org retrieved Dec. 27, 2021.

4. The lawful use of hanging as a method of execution should not be confused with lynching, an unlawful and often vigilante method of murdering individuals.

5. It should be noted that while New Hampshire has abolished the death penalty, the repeal may not apply retroactively, leaving a prisoner on death row still facing possible execution, which could open the door to hanging as a method of execution. Ibid.

6. See the Death Penalty Information Center.

7. In 1920 in Arizona, Eva Dugan was accidentally decapitated during a hanging, which led that state to end death by hanging as their method of execution. See Mark Nothaft, "Dugan caused Arizona to change death by hanging," *Republic, AZ Central*, November 1, 2017. Decapitation was not a rare occurrence.

8. Denno, op. cit., 686; Death Penalty Information Center, June 3, 2002.

9. See Bohm, 155.

10. Robert M. Bohm, *Death Quest*, 5th edition, pp. 200–01 (New York: Routledge, 2017).

11. Ibid.

12. Ibid., 156.

13. *The Annison Star* (Alabama), December 12, 1984. The execution of Mr. Stephens was carried out in Georgia.

14. Ibid., October 16, 1985.

15. *Charlotte Observer*, May 10, 1990.

16. See Inre Kemmler, 136 US 436 (1890).

17. It is worthy of note that then–Nevada governor Emmet Boyle was firmly against capital punishment, but political pressures forced him to concede in signing the Humane Death Bill.

18. By 1937, Arizona, California, Colorado, North Carolina, and Wyoming all had passed legislation using this method of execution; it did not take long for Maryland, Mississippi, Missouri, and New Mexico to follow suit with their own legislation.

19. See *Bucklew versus Precythe*, Slip Opinion No. 17–8151 (2018); *Baze versus Rees*, 553 U.S. 35 (2008): Avoiding all risk of pain is not required by the Eighth Amendment.

20. Oklahoma settling upon lethal injection as their chosen method of execution should not be viewed exclusively through an altruistic desire to make execution less painful for the condemned. The fact is, Oklahoma was substantially motivated by the economic cost of execution. In 1966, when the state legislature was considering their method of execution, legislators noted that the cost of repairing their electric chair was estimated to be $62,000, while the cost of repairing the gas chamber was estimated to be $300,000. But death by lethal injection was estimated to cost approximately fifteen dollars per execution. See Bohm, ibid., 159.

21. L. Koniaris, T. Zimmers, D. Lubarsky, and J. Sheldon (2005). Inadequate anesthesia in lethal injection for execution. *Lancet*, 365, 1412–14.

22. Bohm, 162, citing *The Anniston Star* (Alabama), December 13, 1998.

23. Cited in "Some Doctors Willing to Kill," *Orlando Sentinel*, November 20, 2001, A15.

24. See *Baze versus Rees*, 533 U.S. 35 (2008).

25. While *Furman versus Georgia* briefly outlawed capital punishment based upon the Eighth Amendment's "cruel and unusual" standard, it did not take long for the sanction to be reinstated by the Court's decision in *Gregg versus Georgia*, 428 U.S. 153 (1976).

26. Ibid.

27. For a description of some of these botched efforts at death by lethal injection, see Virginia Hatch and Anthony Walsh, *Capital Punishment: Theory and Practice of the Ultimate Penalty* (Oxford: Oxford University Press, 2016), 146–48.

28. See Denno (2014).

29. Denno, University of Miami Symposium, *The Future of the Death Penalty in America* (2012).

Chapter 6

Bad Lawyers: The Unspoken Key to Many Death Sentences

We have examined constitutional issues, we have looked at the methods we use to conduct our executions, we have considered our history, and we have questioned the financial viability of maintaining such a system. Now we must turn our focus on the very group of individuals who are charged to protect the rights of every person on death row, from initial arrest, through trial, after conviction, and during appeals. This is the capital-defense attorney.

It goes without saying that a good lawyer is an essential component in any legal dispute, civil or criminal. It would be naïve, however, to assume that all lawyers are equal in skill, experience, influence, and ability. While every person in our legal system deserves qualified, competent legal representation, in many mundane legal matters, this difference among lawyers is not something to be overly concerned with. But in the area of capital punishment, this difference can literally mean the difference between life and death.

The inescapable fact is that capital defendants are much less likely to be sentenced to death when represented by qualified attorneys, particularly when those attorneys have the time and resources to present their defense.

Perhaps this fact could not be truer than in the state of Texas, the nation's number-one state for executions. An examination of 461 capital cases by the *Dallas Morning News* found that nearly one in four condemned inmates had been represented at trial or on appeal by court-appointed attorneys who had been disciplined for professional misconduct at some point in their careers. Further, an investigation by the Texas Defender Service found that "death row inmates today face a one-in-three chance of being executed without having the case properly investigated by competent attorneys, and without having any claims of innocence or unfairness presented or heard."[1]

While this is a substantial problem in Texas, this is not just a problem found only in that state. This is a problem that can be found anywhere the death penalty prospers. For example, in Washington state, one-fifth of the eighty-four people who have faced execution in the past twenty years were represented by lawyers who had been, or were later, disbarred, suspended, or arrested. Also consider that according to an investigation by the *Chicago Tribune*, 12 percent of those sentenced to death from 1976 to 1999 were represented by "an attorney who had been, or was later, disbarred or suspended—disciplinary sanctions reserved for conduct so incompetent, unethical or even criminal that the state believes an attorney's license should be taken away." An additional 9.5 percent of inmates "have received a new trial or sentencing because their attorneys' incompetence rendered the verdict or sentence unfair, court records show."[2]

Finally, in North Carolina, at least sixteen death-row inmates, including three who were executed, were represented by lawyers who have been disbarred or disciplined for unethical or criminal conduct.

ILL-EQUIPPED, UNPREPARED, AND UNDERPAID: CAPITAL-DEFENSE COUNSEL

A death-penalty trial is like no other trial in our system of justice. Trials come in numerous forms throughout our judicial system, and the end result can be very serious indeed. We have trials to determine contract rights, trials to decide whether two people will remain married, trials designed to compensate victims for injuries, and of course, throughout our criminal justice system, we have trials to determine guilt or innocence of a crime, where the sentences can range from fines and penalties to incarceration for a set period of time or life. Usually, in all our various criminal trials, we are somewhat unsure of what the final outcome will be for the losing party. In civil cases, the judge or jury will decide what the outcome will be from a range of options, and in criminal cases, the judge decides what the sentence will be from a range of sentencing options. All these factors change in death-penalty cases. In cases where the prosecution is seeking execution, it is known from the very first day of trial that a loss means the end of the defendant's life. This mere fact elevates every stage and every aspect of a capital trial to the highest levels of intensity, with the most responsibility for the outcome falling to the attorney for the capital defendant. Or at least this is how it should be.

When all is said and done, nothing more perfectly guarantees acquittal or the conviction and execution of a capital defendant than the defense counsel who is representing the person to potentially be placed on death row. The decisions, skill, and experience of all defense lawyers are critical to any defense, but for the capital defendant, these factors can literally mean the difference between life and death. Sadly, however, much too often, capital defendants are represented by defense counsel who are ill-equipped, unprepared, and underpaid.[3] In these cases, this poor representation is occurring at the most critical stage of legal representation in our criminal justice system—the death-penalty defense.

THE CAPITAL TRIAL

It is exceptionally important to note that the capital trial is the capital defendant's best opportunity to avoid execution. It is at this trial where the defense can present evidence of mitigating facts, where evidence of mental capacity and mental state can take center stage in the defense. It is during the trial that the capital defendant can introduce exculpatory information that may free him, or where forensic evidence, such as DNA, can not only remove the cloud of guilt hanging over the capital defendant, but also absolutely scientifically exclude the defendant from the possibility of culpability. Conversely, the labyrinthine process of overturning death sentences on appeal requires a herculean and persistent effort far beyond the capabilities and finances of most capital defendants to effectuate.

Given the foregoing, it is exceedingly clear that the capital trial is the most important stage of defense for the capital defendant. Whereas the job of any defense counsel is comprehensive and demanding, this fact is doubly true for the capital defendant. It is not an overstatement to assert that often the only person standing between the capital defendant and the death chamber is the skill and ability of his lawyer. The capital-defense lawyer, from the moment notice is given of an intent to seek the death penalty by the prosecution, must exercise exceptional skill and foresight in preparing for what is literally a life-or-death defense. Additionally, the capital-defense lawyer must recognize that a capital trial is not like other criminal defenses. The trial actually is bifurcated into two very distinct and important phases. It is critical that the capital -defense lawyer is skilled and prepared for each of these two phases.

To be precise, it is important that these two phases are understood. To underscore the importance of each phase, the capital-defense lawyer must know and prepare for the first phase of the trial. This is the part of the proceedings that most of us are familiar with, commonly referred to as the guilt phase. During this phase of the proceedings, the attorney is defending against the charges with the focus on having the capital defendant being found not guilty, either by a judge or by a jury, whichever was elected to hear the case.[4] During this first phase, the ultimate question to be decided is, did he do it or not? Is he guilty as charged, and/or is someone else responsible? Does he have an excuse, such as self-defense, or is he suffering from a mental defect that removes the requisite responsibility for the act, even if he is proven to have committed it? To that end, every effort by the defense attorney should be used to achieve a finding of not guilty or some reduction in guilt. Without a doubt, this is the most important phase of the capital defendant's route through the criminal-justice system, and when done properly, wrongful convictions are prevented, excessive punishment of the guilty is avoided, and more often than not, the guilty receive life sentences rather than death sentences.

However, if the defendant is found guilty as charged, the case moves into a completely unique phase in the capital trial. This second phase is called the "penalty phase," and with rare exceptions, this portion of the proceedings follows immediately after the conclusion of the guilt phase.

During the penalty phase of a capital case, there is one simple question to be answered: "Shall this defendant be put to death?" The capital-defense lawyer must be prepared to demonstrate by clear and convincing evidence that the capital defendant, who has just been found guilty of a horrible crime, is a person whose life is worth saving. It must be proven that the alternative to execution—spending the rest of the defendant's life in jail without the possibility of parole—is the preferred conclusion rather than the execution being sought by the prosecution. The capital-defense lawyer must anticipate and be prepared for both phases of a capital defense. The complexity of each step toward preparation for both phases of a capital trial cannot be understated. The general steps each defense lawyer must take are outlined below.

Pretrial Preparation: The initial stages of a criminal defense are critical to the ultimate success of any defense. During these initial weeks and often months, discovery is obtained from the prosecution, and investigation is conducted by the attorney, the staff, and often private investigators. Motions to help shape the defense are decided upon, filed, and presented. Witnesses are lined up, and experts are often contracted and prepared.

Theory of Defense: For starters, the defense lawyer and her team must decide on a strategy or theory upon which the entire defense will be based. This theory should be based upon evidence that is currently known to exist or is anticipated to be available at the time of trial. The trial lawyer must determine how this evidence will be used to support the defense, as well as contradict the allegations of the prosecution. An inexperienced or unprepared trial lawyer will struggle with the requisite decision-making required to be successful at this point. This is one of the many reasons why an experienced, veteran trial lawyer is much preferred for capital-defense cases.

Witnesses: Not only is the defense lawyer called upon to assess and strategize the use of witnesses, but she must also determine which type of witnesses will be most helpful, the strengths and weaknesses of each witness, and the likelihood of that witness's testimony being controverted

Expert Witnesses: The expert witness is absolutely critical in a death penalty case. These highly trained, educated, and experienced professionals are selected to provide insight into such critical issues as the mental health of the defendant, the accuracy of testimony presented by both defense and prosecution, the instrumentalities of the crime for which the defendant is facing death, the defendant's social history, the relationship this may or may not have had on the crime, and a whole list of other scientific forensic issues that may be presented during a trial. The skillful use of expert witnesses is critical to any defense, but it is absolutely crucial for the defense of a capital defendant. The defense lawyer must be knowledgeable, informed, well-prepared, and financed to be in a position to identify where expert witnesses are needed, determine which experts are best suited to bolster a defense that is consistent with the trial lawyer's theory of defense, and most importantly, arrange for the expert to testify. This means transportation of the expert, lodging, special accommodations, food, payment—often on an hourly basis—for the expert's services, and arranging for the expert to prepare a thorough presentation in advance of the trial. This may include observing evidence, visiting crime scenes, obtaining reports, and interviewing the defendant, among other things.

Jury Selection: Every trial lawyer who has argued in a fair number of trials has a method of selecting juries they utilize. Some do so based upon their own experience, while others will hire jury consultants to aid them in the selection of the "right" jurors. For the well-financed defense counsel, ideally both are utilized. The selection of jurors is incredibly important to the outcome of the defense, and failing to select jurors properly can often doom the defendant.

Presentation: The ultimate job of the defense lawyer is to take all the available tools, information, facts, opinions, and evidence and present them during the trial in a manner that is understandable, is persuasive, and compels the acquittal or the elimination of the imposition of a sentence of death. The capital-defense trial lawyer must understand the two phases of a capital trial (the guilt and penalty phases) and be adept at presenting the proper defense at each stage. The capital-trial lawyer must understand that in most cases, the jury will determine guilt or innocence and the judge will determine the sentence, and they must be prepared to be persuasive to both completely different audiences. This ability to present a defense is an evolving skill that is acquired over time and relies heavily on experience, training, and most importantly, preparation. In order to be effective, the trial lawyer must be properly motivated to provide excellent representation, must be prepared and well-informed, and must possess a certain degree of skill. It has been said by experienced trial lawyers that no really capable trial lawyer should ever lose a capital case.[5]

As can be seen, the role of the capital-defense lawyer is multifaceted, demanding, and crucial to the successful and equitable defense of the defendant facing the death penalty. A drop-off in skill, and/or ability, at any of these crucial phases will almost certainly doom the capital defendant to execution.

Sadly, most capital defendants do not have the requisite level of defense and legal representation, and their death sentences are fairly predictable, not due to the crime committed, but the quality of lawyer assigned to represent them.

THE CAPITAL-DEFENSE LAWYER

It was important to describe what a capital-defense lawyer should be so it can be understood how rare this quality of lawyer is for the death-row defendant and how startlingly inadequate most capital defenses are. In what is arguably the most important type of defense in our criminal-justice system, the defense that will ultimately determine literal life or death, the level of defense is inexcusably poor and inadequate much too often. No appellate court should ever take lightly the appellate argument focusing on the ineffective assistance of trial counsel,[6] yet this form of appellate attack is routinely dismissed out of hand. No appeal to a governor, *habeas corpus* petition, or appeal to the United States Supreme Court, based upon a claim of ineffective assistance of counsel, should ever be summarily disregarded. Yet much too often, they are. Cases should not proceed without thorough investigation, and the capital-trial counsel should be held to the highest standard of all criminal-defense counsel, given the devastating consequences that will certainly be the result if they are not. Life is a fundamental right guaranteed by the Constitution, and the taking of life by governmental authority should insist upon the highest standard of care before ever being considered as an option.

BAD LAWYERS: ACTUAL CASES

Death rows around the nation are littered with defendants who would not be there but for the inadequacy of the lawyers who defended them. In fact, the quality of representation is so low that literally novice lawyers with barely any legal experience are better able to defend these defendants than the lawyers who have been engaged to do so. In the words of South Carolina trial lawyer David Bruck, "no one who has any money, faces the death penalty." Consider, for example, these cases:

Nine years after John Young was condemned to death in Georgia, his disbarred lawyer, Charles Marchman, admitted that his drug use, the breakup of his marriage, the discovery of his homosexuality, and other factors prevented him from defending Young adequately. Notwithstanding, when these issues were raised on appeal, the Court ruled that the conviction should stand.

James Copeland, on Louisiana death row, had a lawyer at his second trial who confessed that he'd never read the first trial's transcript and did little to uncover evidence supporting life in prison over execution. This complete failure of his attorney to vigorously defend him absolutely led to his ultimate execution.

Texas lawyer John Wood unsuccessfully defended Jesus Romero against the death penalty with twenty-nine words, among them was this woefully inadequate presentation: "You've got the man's life in your hands, you can take it or not. That's all I have to say."[7]

Even sleeping during the trial is not enough to prove ineffective counsel. John Benn of Houston, Texas, referred to a capital case as "boring" while admitting during a recess that he was, in fact, asleep. So, too, did the late Joe Frank Cannon, in representing Calvin Burdine. His case was overturned on appeal, and a new trial was ordered because he was asleep so often and for such significant periods of time so as to deprive the defendant of adequate counsel. His other client was not so lucky; when Carl Johnson appealed, complaining of his attorney being asleep, the appellate court denied that he was the victim of ineffective counsel "notwithstanding the sleeping lawyer"[8]

Herman Alcantor has been called the busiest capital-defense lawyer in the entire United States. (This is not a compliment.) Capital cases are complex and time-consuming. One case can be an entire caseload for the capital-defense attorney, and almost all agree it is not a good idea to handle more than two at a time. In 2009, Alcantar was counsel for five at one time. In the defense of Fabio Gomez, he was so busy that even though it was a month before trial, he had not filed a single substantive motion, nor had he visited his client for over a year! Six of his trial clients were convicted and are now sitting on death row awaiting execution.[9]

In another of Alcantar's cases, he presented his entire mitigation case in one afternoon and one morning. However, this pales in comparison to his purported representation of Brian Womble, in which Alcantor inexplicably elected to present no mitigation case at all. On appeal of Brian's conviction, his new and competent lawyers found these factors in mitigation that should have been presented either during the guilt phase or the penalty phase of the trial:

1. Brian was born addicted to heroin due to his mother's addiction.
2. As a child, he had been thrown down steps, beaten with a broomstick, and slammed in the head by a wooden fence. This type of injury could easily account for personality deficiencies and the inability to fully appreciate the consequences of his actions.
3. He stuttered and suffered from head trauma.
4. He had indications of suffering from fetal alcohol syndrome.
5. His mother was mentally ill and a heroin addict.

6. He suffered from paranoid delusions, hallucinations, and depression, and he had tried to kill himself.
7. Hours before the crime that landed him on death row, he checked himself into a mental-health facility saying he wanted to kill himself and possibly others—yet he was permitted to leave. Hours later, he broke into a home and sadly killed two sleeping victims.

Alcantar did not present any of these facts in mitigation. When one juror found out about these additional facts, he said that had he known, he would have voted for life instead of death, "no doubt about it."[10]

The case of Ron Williamson, a death-row exoneration case made famous by legendary author and lawyer John Grisham, details the tragic consequences of a wrongful conviction aided in large part by ineffective counsel. In his book *The Innocent Man: Murder and Injustice in a Small Town*,[11] Grisham shares the story of how Mr. Williamson's counsel presented a totally inadequate defense, with the trial lasting only two days. During his trial, hair evidence was introduced to link him to the crime. This type of evidence is universally regarded as unreliable "junk science." No evidence of his deteriorating mental health was introduced by his counsel, nor was a motion made to assess his competence to stand trial. Perhaps most disturbing was the admission as his "confession" the recitation of a dream he had been coerced to tell, which was then used as a false confession. In a strange twist of fate, it was later revealed that the actual murderer was used as a key witness for the prosecution.[12]

Texas lawyer Jerry Guerinot, seventy-one, announced in 2016 that he was "retiring" from death-penalty cases. He made it clear that he was not retiring from practicing law, just from defending death-penalty clients. He cited his displeasure over all the criticism he has endured for his death-penalty cases over the years as a motivating factor in his decision to retire as a capital-defense lawyer. In a four-decade career of representing defendants facing the death penalty, Guerinot lost every one of his almost three dozen cases, which he attributed to his decision to repeatedly take "notorious cases" rather than his lack of skill and commitment. This is a dubious claim at best. In one seven-month span, Guerinot completed four separate death-penalty cases. When considering this legal feat, Jim Marcus, the co-director of the capital-punishment clinic at the University of Texas, said, "To do so is unthinkable, given the complexity and time demands of a single case." Marcus, a veteran defense lawyer, is representing one of Guerinot's former clients on appeal. As part of his appeal, Marcus is citing Guerinot's failure to adequately represent the capital defendant as one of the grounds for overturning the death sentence.[13]

Some opponents of the death penalty label Guerinot as the worst lawyer in America. He has been roundly criticized for failing to prepare adequately, failing to question witnesses, and in one particular case he lost, he did not meet with his client until one month prior to the trial, and during the trial, he failed to mention that the defendant, a female British citizen, was from a country where the death penalty is outlawed. He also failed to contact the British consulate, and he failed to question the court's jurisdiction over a British subject. All these facts would have been highly significant if not completely dispository.

If skill were the only problem, we could probably come up with better solutions more easily, but the problem is much worse than the skill of the defense attorney. The fact is, defending capital cases is expensive, and most capital defendants are also indigent. As a result, they must often rely upon court-appointed attorneys. Court-appointed defense counsel rarely has the resources to mount a credible defense. For example, in the 1990s, attorneys in Alabama were being paid only twenty dollars an hour for out-of-court time in capital cases with a limit of two thousand dollars per case. Mississippi was limiting payments to one thousand dollars per case, and as late as 2004, Florida had a cap of thirty-five hundred dollars per case. This includes expert and witness fees as well as attorney's fees. It is not uncommon for lawyers handling capital cases in Alabama, Georgia, Mississippi, and Virginia (leading states for capital executions) to pay capital-defense lawyers less than their state's respective minimum wage. In fact, many states have been known to appoint lawyers who submit the lowest bids for this type of legal representation. Typically, no lawyer with ability, experience, and a high level of skill is willing to work for these wages unless they are doing so for the good of mankind rather than a principle of sound business.

In 1924, famed attorney Clarence Darrow observed that "no Court ever interferes with a good lawyer's business by calling him in to, and compelling him to, give time" to a poor person facing criminal charges; instead, judges appoint lawyers willing to take the case for what the courts pay.[14]

THE INCREDIBLE ADVANTAGE OF THE PROSECUTION OVER THE DEFENSE

If there was ever a place where a fair and equitable proceeding is called for, with both sides of the debate having the same access to tools, personnel, and resources, it is in the arena of capital punishment. After all, there is quite literally, and specifically, a life at stake. Even more, the potential of the state actually taking a life in the wrong manner is in itself a crime against all humanity and a human-rights violation. The social contract and the concept of *parens patriae* prohibits the state from doing harm to its citizens without just cause, yet we allow this gross violation to exist, unfettered and unchecked.

No stronger argument need be made than to look at the one-sided advantage the prosecution holds over the capital-defense lawyer.

Long before the case ever comes to trial, long before the case is certified as a capital case, the investigation has already begun for the prosecution. Facts are being determined, and evidence is being collected by the prosecution long before the defense even knows a case will be filed. It is not unusual for a prosecutor to have access to actual crime scenes months before the defense even knows their client is being targeted. At the same time that prosecutors have access to actual evidence and crime scenes, the defense is reduced to viewing photographs and reading narratives of how the evidence was discovered and collected. This is a tremendous advantage for the prosecution from the very start, but there is so much more.

For example, the lawyers in the prosecutor's office spend years specializing in one very specific thing—criminal law. Often there is a specialty within this specialty, i.e., prosecuting capital cases. These lawyers have stable incomes, health benefits, and retirement plans, which, in some instances, afford them the opportunity to spend their entire careers doing this one job. Additionally, there is an investment in these lawyers to ensure they are well trained and kept abreast of the latest developments in their specialty areas. They attend conferences, participate in continuing legal education programs, and are encouraged to conduct research and participate in in-house training programs. This type of investment produces well-trained, topflight, seasoned prosecutors, capable of presenting very persuasive cases when arguing for the death penalty.

This would be enough to give a tremendous advantage to the prosecutors, but it does not end there. Each of these prosecutors has at his immediate disposal an endless amount of free investigative services to help bolster their cases. This comes in the form of local police officers, and it can include special investigators, the FBI, DEA agents, county and state law-enforcement officers, and more, all marshalled to aid the prosecutor in delivering a death sentence in capital cases.

It is clear to see the advantage is almost insurmountable, but there is even more. The prosecutor's office has within its reach a wide range of experts who can help shape the case for the prosecutors long before trial and certainly during the trial. Mental-health professionals, ballistic experts, crime-scene analysts, DNA experts, profilers, medical examiners, crime labs, and virtually every kind and type of expert imaginable all work in concert to assist the prosecutor in winning her case—at no cost to the prosecution.[15]

The benefits outlined above exist once the case is filed as a capital case and continue throughout the trial and into conviction. But once the sentence of death is pronounced, these highly trained prosecutors are done with the case and can move on to the next one. However, any defendant who appeals their death sentence, via appeal or any form of mandatory review, must now face a new squad of prosecutors, typically the attorney general's office. These prosecutors have a special division designed to manage all appeals of death sentences. They are highly skilled appellate lawyers, well-financed, well-compensated, and well-trained, with access to their own set of experts, specialists, crime labs, and mental-health/social-work professionals. Once again, paying for these resources is not the concern of the lawyers working on the appeal; it is funded by taxpayers and is part of the overall budget for these offices.

THE FINAL PROSECUTION ADVANTAGE

Finally, there is one last advantage that may not immediately appear to be significant, but that carries within it the crushing and final blow to the capital-defense lawyer. This advantage is the existence of long-standing working relationships with judges, police officers, clerks, expert witnesses, and every expert associated with the conviction of the defendant. This advantage manifests itself in a variety of ways, such as familiarity with expert witnesses who have been used countless times in countless cases. The flow of direct examination and the anticipation of cross-examination is all familiar terrain to be traversed by the expert and the prosecution. The relationship between the prosecution and the judges is also in play; often the same judge and prosecutor have worked in the same courtroom for years. This not only breeds a working relationship, but it also allows the prosecution to be aware of the judge's proclivities and tendencies, which, as any trial lawyer can attest, is invaluable information.

With the exception of the judge, probably the most important person in the courtroom work group is the judge's clerk. This person knows the judge's schedule, knows the judge's personal habits, sets hearings and motions on behalf of counsel, and is the general gatekeeper between the lawyers and the machinations of the court. Having a strong working relationship with this person is a prize to be sought and coveted, which most prosecutors enjoy simply by virtue of having been in the courtroom repeatedly.

Conversely, compare the foregoing with the experience of the capital-defense lawyer, who may or may not be appearing in this courtroom for the first time, perhaps the only time. He has no working relationship with the courtroom work group, and he is viewed as an outsider at best and the "enemy" at worst. Before the trial ever begins, the capital-defense lawyer is fighting an uphill battle. It is a tribute to the dedicated lawyers who practice in this area that, given these odds, a capital defense is ever successful.

What should be abundantly clear by now is that if we genuinely wanted a fair system of justice, we would even the playing field between the prosecution and the defense. By doing so, the injustices that occur in this area of law could be drastically reduced. Instead, however, the odds have been stacked mightily in favor of the prosecution. With this being the case, how can we ever rely upon a final verdict and a mandated execution as having been just? Rhetorically responding, we cannot. Capital punishment is fatally flawed and must be abolished.

> Even now, are not all imaginative and humane people shocked at the spectacle of a killing by the state? How many men and women would be willing to act as executioners? How many fathers and mothers would want their children to witness an official killing? What kind of people read the sensational reports of an execution? If all right-thinking men and women were not ashamed of it, why would it be needful that judges and lawyers and preachers apologize for the barbarity? How can the state censure the cruelty of the man who—moved by strong passions, or acting to save his freedom, or influenced by weakness or fear—takes human life when everyone knows that the state itself, after long premeditation and settled hatred, not only kills, but first tortures and bedevils its victims for weeks with the impending doom?—*Clarence Darrow, The Forum*, September 1928[16]

NOTES

1. See *Lethal Indifference*, Report of the Texas Defender Service (2002), https://texasdefender.org.
2. Ken Armstrong and Steve Mills, "Inept Defenses Cloud Verdict," *Chicago Tribune*, November 15, 1999.
3. See *Death Quest III*, 257.
4. In criminal cases, it is the defendant's right to elect trial by a jury or to waive the right to trial by jury and have the case decided by a judge. When a judge takes on the role of a jury, this is referred to as a "bench trial."
5. See *Death Quest III*, 257.
6. The "ineffective assistance of counsel" is a typical and usually unsuccessful appellate claim that many defendants allege after losing at trial. Far too many appellate courts dismiss this claim as legitimate grounds for reversal, failing to acknowledge just how fundamentally salient this claim may be. In a capital defense, careful consideration should be given to any such claims, and they should never summarily be disregarded. Far too often, these types of claims are true.
7. "Quality of Justice," *Dallas Morning News*, November 10, 2000.
8. Ibid.
9. Texas Defender Service, *Lethal Indifference: The Fatal Combination of Incompetent Attorneys and Unaccountable Courts* (2002).

10. *Seattle Post-Intelligencer*, August 6, 2001.

11. John, Grisham, *The Innocent Man: Murder and Injustice in a Small Town* (New York: Double Day Publishing, 2006).

12. Ibid.

13. Michael Graczyk, "Texas lawyer who lost all death penalty cases says he's done," Associated Press (August 13, 2016), FoxNews.com, retrieved June 29, 2023.

14. See Bohm, *Death Quest III*, 3rd ed. (Newark, NJ: Matthew Bender and Company, 2006) 258–60.

15. Certainly there is a cost associated with these services, but these costs are absorbed in the overall budget of the prosecution's office, or the offices of the agency being used, and are paid by taxpayers. Unlike the defense lawyer, these expenses are not a direct concern of the individual prosecutor.

16. Clarence Darrow, *The Forum*, September 1928, reprinted in *Clarence Darrow: Verdicts Out of Court* (Chicago, Ill.: Elephant Paperback, 1963), 231–32.

Chapter 7

The Persistent Problem of False Confessions in Death Penalty Cases

We have looked at several external factors that have led to the execution of capital defendants. We have examined the role that bad lawyers play in capital cases. We have looked at the horrific methods of execution employed, and we have even measured the cost of administering this type of criminal sanction. However, sometimes the capital defendant himself is to blame for his predicament and would not be on death row but for the one thing he did, even though otherwise innocent. This is when the defendant falsely confesses to a crime that he did not commit. False confessions occur with too much regularity in criminal cases, and while they are somewhat rare in capital cases, it is still often enough to be a significant problem, wherever it is found to have happened.

A false confession in any criminal case is a significant problem; however, when it occurs in a capital-punishment case, the effects can be devastating, and a permanent miscarriage of justice can occur. There are several factors that significantly contribute to the incidence of wrongful convictions, and false confessions is one of the main ones. Innocence projects around the nation have worked tirelessly to exonerate the innocent as well as identify the causes of wrongful convictions in hopes of preventing their reoccurrence. Some of the major contributing factors leading to wrongful convictions have been identified as:

1. Eyewitness misidentification;
2. Unqualified or disinterested defense counsel;
3. Misconduct by prosecutors; and at the core of the problem; and
4. False confessions.

In this chapter, we will take a look at the causes, circumstances, and effects of false confessions generally, with particular emphasis on death-penalty cases specifically. We will also look at suggestions and recommendations to lessen the occurrence of false confessions.

INNOCENCE IS CENTRAL TO OUR SYSTEM OF JUSTICE, AND CLAIMS OF INNOCENCE SHOULD NOT BE TAKEN LIGHTLY

Claims of innocence are not uncommon in our criminal-justice system. As a system of justice, there is no greater claim one can make than to claim innocence. In fact, our system of justice is predicated on the very presumption that every person, no matter the charge, no matter what their background may be, and no matter what the circumstances are, is presumed innocent until proven guilty. Further, this presumption of innocence travels with every single person throughout the circuitous criminal justice process until a judge, jury, or the individual via plea agreement or confession declares them guilty beyond a reasonable doubt.[1]

The presumption of innocence is so sacrosanct that we have constructed our rules of procedure, jury instructions, evidentiary processes, codifications, and case law to protect the rights of the innocent at all costs, even if in doing so, some factually guilty individuals may, in fact, be found legally not guilty.[2] This principle of justice, borrowed from legendary jurist Sir William Blackstone, has been consistently applied as a guiding principle of justice in the American criminal courts.

Understandably, as a result of this ultra-care and concern for the pre-conviction innocent, it is understandable that perhaps less concern exists for the post-conviction defendant as the presumption shifts from pre-conviction innocence to post-conviction guilt. Notwithstanding this shift of presumption, we hold out one last safety net for those who may have been found guilty erroneously—the appellate process.

Through the use of the appellate process, it is the hope that legal errors can be exposed and ideally corrected, thus further protecting the innocent from the legal tragedy of being found guilty of a charge they did not commit. Given these safeguards, why, then, should we be so very concerned with those who profess their innocence after trial? Aren't these claims of innocence typically unfounded and a drain on our already-overburdened judicial system? Or does this system recognize the inherent shortcomings as acceptable ones with which we can live?[3]

These are all valid questions that deserve an answer. The fact is, conviction of the innocent is a growing problem that has become an untenable stain on our criminal-justice system. As the great trial lawyer Clarence Darrow once said, when it comes to innocence in our criminal justice system, "great tragedies have been committed and [others] often barely averted to avoid even greater tragedy."[4] As the public becomes aware of case after case of factually innocent individuals being convicted and serving long sentences for crimes they did not commit, the outcry has increased. Many lawyers have dedicated their careers to exonerating the wrongfully convicted; Innocence Projects have sprung up across the country; and public officials and governors have declared an end to the death penalty because of the increasing unreliability of guilty verdicts and defendant's self-professed claims of guilt. What was once a little-known fact among lawyers, judges, professors, and researchers has been thrust to the forefront of public discussions regarding the state of our criminal-justice system. Books have been written and movies have been made exposing this problem to mainstream America. Now the questions have become: What is the cause of this problem, and how can we fix it?

To answer these questions, we must take a look at our system of justice and assess what we theoretically value most. To that end, we should be able to agree that our criminal-justice system has two overriding goals, and each is of equal importance: They are: 1) protect the innocent, and 2) convict the guilty. These goals are frustrated when the innocent are convicted and the guilty go free. How, then, does this occur? What would cause the innocent to be convicted? One answer is a false confession by the defendant.

FALSE CONFESSIONS

Why would anyone confess to a crime they did not commit? In particular, why would anyone confess to a capital crime? Underlying these questions is the presumption of what logically follows such an inquiry—i.e., if someone did confess to a crime, then we should take them at their word and assume they must have actually committed the crime. This is not only a logical conclusion to reach, but a reasonable inference to draw. However, upon closer examination, there are, in fact, several reasons an accused person would confess to a crime they did not commit.[5] There are certain types of individuals who are prone to make such confessions; they are:

(a) The Mentally Impaired

Our criminal-justice system is routinely populated by those individuals suffering from mental defects and disorders of diverse types. While individual defects may not rise to the level of the legal definition of *insanity*,[6] the mental impairment creates a circumstance that can lead to a false confession. Often, these defendants are easily influenced, have a will that is easily manipulated, and have an unreasonable desire to please others.[7] In general, these individuals are too mentally malleable to provide reliable testimony or legally sufficient admissions of guilt.[8]

(b) Minors and the Under-Aged

In our legal system, minors are not allowed to enter legally binding contracts, are not allowed to enter the armed service, and are not allowed to vote, drink alcohol, smoke, or enter a matrimonial agreement.[9] Most telling, in our criminal-justice system, minors are not allowed to be executed for their crimes.[10] All these rules and restrictions exist to protect minors and the underaged because there is the common recognition that these individuals are in no position to make sound, reasonable decisions or judgments on their own.[11] Consider, for example, the following case:

> Sixteen-year-old Felix (last name intentionally omitted) was arrested for the murder of Antonio (last name omitted) in Oakland, California. Felix was frightened, isolated, and in an interrogation room, late at night. He was not allowed to speak to an attorney, and his requests to see his mother were denied. Prosecutors verbally accosted him, harangued him, and questioned him incessantly until he told them what they wanted to hear. He tried to describe how he committed the crime, and when his description was wrong, interviewers fed him the proper responses. After hours of questioning and "suggestions" for altering his story, his confession was taped and presented as evidence. The one factor that saved him from conviction at trial was the revelation that the date of the crime was a date when Felix was incarcerated in a juvenile-detention facility.[12]

Felix was fortunate—his airtight alibi saved him from a wrongful conviction. But too often, no such alibi exists, particularly when it comes to minors. Because of their easy manipulation, any confession by a minor should, at the very least, be viewed with great suspicion and in need of independent corroboration, and, at the very least, be considered unreliable. To the contrary, however, the record is replete with convictions of minors, based upon their own confessions.

(c) The Easily Misled

Some individuals are easily manipulated for a variety of reasons. Consider the case of Eddie Lowery, who lost ten years of his life for a crime he did not commit.[13] In his case, there was no physical evidence presented at trial linking him to the crime of rape, but there was one overwhelming piece of evidence presented by the prosecution that could not be overcome: Eddie's confession.[14] His confession was detailed, accurate, and consistent with facts the prosecutors alleged only the true perpetrator could have known. If not for DNA evidence proving the impossibility of his guilt, Mr. Lowery might never have been exonerated. "I beat myself up a lot about having confessed," Mr. Lowery said in an interview. "I thought I was the only dummy who did that."[15]

However, Eddie Lowery's confession is not that rare. In his book *Convicting the Innocent: Where Criminal Prosecutions Go Wrong*, Brandon Garrett, a professor at the University of Virginia Law School, noted that since 1976, over forty other individual have confessed to crimes, confessions that DNA evidence would later show to be false.[16] Psychologists have explained that the constant questioning and high-pressure tactics, coupled with feelings of having no way out and no lawyer present, are all contributing factors.[17] In Eddie Lowrey's case, he explained it this way: "I didn't see any way out except to tell them what they wanted to hear and then get a lawyer to prove my innocence."

(d) False Admissions due to Police Tactics

The police have very powerful tools at their disposal for extracting confessions. While interrogating, they often confuse and disorient the suspect to their advantage. A perfect example of this is the tragic case of Ron Williamson. During his interrogation, the police asked Ron to recall a dream he had about the murder victim. They then turned his description of the dream he'd had into a confession. This was done all while the police knew he suffered from mental-health problems. The description he gave was used as his "confession" at trial, which ultimately led to his conviction for a murder he did not commit. Ron spent eleven years on death row before finally being exonerated by the Innocence Project.[18]

It is not uncommon for members of law enforcement to mislead, or even lie, about the existence of physical evidence, the existence of witnesses, or statements that have purportedly been given by others implicating the suspect. Many interrogators are skilled at playing on a suspect's biases, fears, loyalties, and lack of knowledge. Even more, some have been known to use violence and torture to induce confessions. While we must recognize the need for law enforcement to use every legal means at their disposal to convict the guilty, we must also recognize that these same tools may be used to convict the innocent, as well.

(e) Jailhouse "Snitches," or Informants

More often than most would care to acknowledge, perjury is used when a confidential informant or jailhouse snitch comes forward to reveal the alleged confession of a cellmate. It is incredible the number of times that a circumstantial case is sealed by the so-called confession of the defendant to his cellmate, the informant. It is almost laughable how defendants will protest their innocence for months, even years, to any and all who will listen, but after only a few days of sharing a cell, we are led to believe that this same defendant will feel compelled to change his story and give his cellmate what amounts to a full, detailed confession, which the cellmate, then, out of "civic responsibility" feels the need to come forward and recite. The fact that this informant receives a reduced sentence, has charges dropped, or is on the receiving end of some other significant benefit is overlooked or ignored. The disingenuity of it all is at times sickening, but yet it and has led to numerous convictions of innocent persons.[19]

(f) False Admissions to Obtain a Lesser Charge or Sentence

One of the cornerstones of our criminal justice system is plea bargaining. Without plea bargaining, our courtrooms would be even more overcrowded, and the system would be hopelessly backlogged. The good that can come from an effective plea-bargaining system is that it can free up what would otherwise be wasted time in proving the obvious. By avoiding trials when the outcome is certain, prosecutors, defense counsel, judges, witnesses, and juries are free to devote their time to other matters where the outcome is less certain, and guilt or innocence is not a foregone conclusion.

The bad that comes from our plea-bargaining system is that when innocent defendants believe they have no chance to prove their innocence, accepting a plea to a lesser charge or offense becomes the easy way out and superficially logical.[20]

> The problem here is twofold. First, innocent defendants are forced to choose between pursuing justice and an inevitable conviction. Second, those who accept plea bargains believing they can somehow obtain justice after the fact are usually startled to find that in accepting a plea, they have waived appellate rights, waived any right to a new trial, and waived the right to challenge the sentence imposed after accepting the plea. For the post-conviction defendant who is innocent, this leaves virtually no chance of ever being exonerated from a wrongful conviction.

This problem is even more acute in capital cases. Because of the very real danger of being executed, some innocent individuals charged with death-eligible crimes will plead guilty to lesser, non–death-eligible offenses. In his book *In Spite of Innocence: Erroneous Convictions in Capital Cases*, Professor Michael Radelet found sixteen cases of innocent defendants in the twentieth century who pleaded guilty to noncapital murder to avoid the possibility of execution.[21]

WHERE DO WE GO FROM HERE?

With the incidence of wrongful convictions creating such extreme hardships for those victimized by this legal malady, it is clear we must do more to prevent their occurrence. Those involved in the administration of our criminal-justice system must make additions and adjustments to improve our system of justice. Here are some suggestions for improving our system of justice to prevent wrongful convictions, particularly in capital cases:

Improve the Quality of Defense Attorneys

At the forefront of this battle for those who have been wrongfully charged with crimes they did not commit is the defense counsel. The quality and training of defense attorneys must improve.[22] Defense counsel must not only receive additional training to recognize the potential of a false confession, but they must also be prepared to have the confession excluded from evidence when the facts and circumstances suggest that the confession may, in fact, be tainted.

Moreover, due to the specific nature of allegations of wrongful convictions, it is recommended that all claims of wrongful convictions be reviewed by state-funded agencies created to examine and litigate claims of wrongful convictions on behalf of all defendants, not just indigent ones. It is the obligation of the state to dispense justice fairly and impartially, and when an injustice is claimed, it is the state's burden to identify and correct the injustice.

Remove Time, Jurisdictional, and Other Restrictions on Claims of Innocence

Claims of factual innocence should immediately move into a separate category of posttrial proceedings. All time limits and restrictions on the presentation of new evidence should be removed, and the presumption of innocence should reattach to the post-conviction defendant.[23] It is absolutely untenable to prevent evidence of actual innocence that could potentially exonerate a wrongfully convicted defendant being barred due to time limitations, or restrictive new evidence rules. We must remove all barriers in order to pursue justice.

Improve Police Investigations, Interrogations, and Handling of Evidence

Law-enforcement techniques and tactics must improve with a design to arrest and convict the right person as opposed to convicting the targeted person. Furthermore, confessions by an in-custody defendant should trigger a specific inquiry into the nature and circumstances of the confession, as well as the background profile of the confessor.[24]

Additionally, a series of questions should be answered before a statement purported to be a confession is submitted as evidence. These questions should delve into the circumstances of the confession, the length of time the confessor is in custody prior to the confession, the psychological profile of the confessor, whether the confessor knew details of the crime independent of law enforcement's provision of information, who was present during the confession, whether an offer of favorable treatment was used as an inducement for confession, and more. Finally, the presumption of innocence should remain post-confession.

Law-Enforcement Personnel Involved in Procuring False Confessions Should Be Subjected to Harsh Penalties Including Mandatory Jail Sentences

The damage done to individuals victimized by wrongful convictions can be horrendously immeasurable. Not only have these innocent people spent years, sometimes even decades, incarcerated, but families are torn apart, mental-health issues are created, jobs are lost, and in far too many instances, taxpayers are forced to pay millions of dollars in compensation. Further, the real perpetrator is often left unpursued. Any member of law enforcement who actively and knowingly participates in the creation of a wrongful conviction should stand in judgment for the criminal conspiracy in which they were a participant.[25]

Rigorous Standards Should Be Set for the Use of Jailhouse Snitches and Informants

In far too many instances, jailhouse snitches have been used as instruments to convict the innocent. Significant changes must be made in the use of these types of informants. First, it is suggested that a legal presumption should exist that the informant is unreliable, and if there is no other independent corroborating testimony or evidence, such information should be excluded. Any agreements that are made between the prosecution and the informant should be presented in court, in writing, and under oath, carrying penalties of perjury, and said agreement should be limited to said document, exclusively. Further, this written agreement should be submitted to the defense as part of the pretrial discovery, or the testimony should be excluded.

Additionally, trial judges should inform jurors of the potential hazards of relying on the testimony of jailhouse snitches. Finally, the information provided by a jailhouse snitch/informant should never be the sole basis for the imposition of the death penalty.[26]

REQUIRE DNA TESTING WHERE RELEVANT

Numerous wrongfully convicted defendants have been exonerated via DNA testing after providing a false confession. DNA testing should become mandatory in all cases where DNA exists and where the existence of DNA could prove or disprove guilt.[27] The testing should be done in a reasonable period of time, and the state and federal governments should maintain adequate funds to provide this service.[28]

CONCLUSION

The problem of false confessions is an ongoing one. It is not as uncommon as what may originally have been presumed. The goal of the criminal-justice system should be to convict the guilty and protect the innocent. In order to do this, we must reduce, and hopefully permanently eliminate, wrongful convictions based upon false confessions, particularly when they involve capital punishment.

NOTES

1. See C. Darrow, *Verdicts Out of Court* (1963), 302–14.
2. This principle was first extolled by English jurist Sir William Blackstone, when he said, “Better ten guilty persons escape than one innocent suffer”; the 10:1 ratio has since become known as the “Blackstone ration,” but more specifically, a principle of justice. See Sir William Blackstone, *Commentaries on the Laws of England* (1765).
3. See Johnnie Cochran and David Fisher, *A Lawyer's Life* (New York: Thomas Dunne Books, an imprint of St. Martin’s Press, 2002).

4. See Darrow, *Attorney for the Damned* (New York: Vintage Books, a Division of Random House, [1957] 2011), 270.

5. See James R. Acker and Allison Redlich, *Wrongful Conviction: Law, Science, and Policy* (Carolina Academic Press: 2011), 141-–50.

6. Best described by the McNaughton rule, which, in essence, states: "That by reason of mental defect or disease the defendant is unable to distinguish right from wrong nor conform himself thereto." *United Kingdom House of Lords Decisions. Daniel M'Naghten's Case* (May 26, June 19, 1843), British and Irish Information Institute.

7. Grisham (2006), 100–75.

8. See Allison Redlich and Gail Goodman (2003), "Taking Responsibility for a Crime Not Committed: The Influence of Age and Suggestibility," *Law and Human Behavior* 27, 141–56.

9. Ibid., 141.

10. See *Roper versus Simmons* (2005), ibid.

11. See Gould (2010).

12. See David Shipler, "Why Do Innocent People Confess?" February 23, 2012, *New York Times*, Sunday Review, Opinion Page, www.nytimes.com, retrieved December 12, 2013.

13. See www.msnbc.com/whyinnocentpeopleconfess.

14. See Acker (2011), 141–69.

15. Quoted in "Confessing to Crime, but Innocent," wwwnodeathpenalty.org/ . . . /confessing-crime-innocent, September 13, 2010. Note: Mr. Lowery was eventually awarded 7.5 million dollars for his wrongful conviction.

16. See Garrett (2011), 76–80.

17. See Kassin (2008), 249.

18. For a complete telling of the Ron Williamson saga, see John Grisham, *An Innocent Man: Murder in a Small Town*, in which he detailed Ron's wrongful conviction, death sentence, and eventual exoneration.

19. See Myrna S. Raeder, "See No Evil: Wrongful Convictions and the Prosecutorial Ethics of Offering Testimony of Jailhouse Informants and Dishonest Experts," 76 *Fordham Law Review* (2007), 1413, 1419–20.

20. See Garrett, Ibid., 55.

21. See Radelet et al. (1992).

22. See Darrow, ibid. (1963), 313–24.

23. Material in this section may be found at the Innocence Project website: www.innocenceproject.org.

24. See Findley (2006), 292.

25. See Roach (2010), 89–95.

26. See Bohm, ibid. (2012), 273.

27. See Drizin (2004), 891.

28. See Bohm (2012), 273.

Chapter 8

Wrongful Convictions, Innocence, and the Death Penalty

Perhaps there is no greater injustice known to mankind than to sentence someone to death for a crime they did not commit. The possibility of executing an innocent person has been a historical fact since the execution of Jesus Christ. The record is replete with case after case of factually innocent individuals being exonerated from death row, often mere days or even hours before their appointed time with the executioner. This factor alone has caused governors, legislators, and the public at large to reconsider the viability of capital punishment as a government-sponsored punitive sanction. Whether one is in favor of the death penalty or not, all right- thinking individuals should be opposed to the killing of an innocent person.

Further, we can take no solace in the position that few mistakes are made in this area. There are simply too many factors that play too large of a role in determining whether an individual receives the death penalty or not, and few, if any, of these factors have anything to do with the guilt or innocence of the defendant. There can be no doubt that the most compelling reason for abolishing the continued use of the death penalty is the very real possibility of executing an innocent person for a crime they did not commit. Executing the innocent is a "bell that cannot be unrung" and an error that can never be corrected. The recent attention to this problem has come on the heels of massive attention being paid to exonerations from death row. Legal scholars, lawyers, activists, and even former prosecutors have weighed in on this topic, with many recognizing the implicit danger of executing an innocent man. Legendary fiction author John Grisham was so moved after reading the obituary of an innocent man exonerated from death row, only to die five years later, that he wrote his first nonfiction book about the heartbreaking case of Ron Williamson, who came within hours of being executed before finally being exonerated.[1]

Academy award–winning actress Hilary Swank starred in a movie detailing the true story of Betty Anne Waters, who, after finding no one willing to fight to prove her brother's innocence, courageously put herself through college and law school to defend her brother, wrongfully convicted of murder. She ultimately won his freedom after he had served eighteen years on death row.[2]

In fact, the problem of wrongful convictions in death-penalty cases has become so pervasive that several governors have signed legislation abolishing the death penalty in what was, until that time, a death-penalty state. Perhaps former Illinois governor George Ryan said it best when he initially declared a moratorium on executions in Illinois: "Until I can be sure that everyone sentenced to death in Illinois is truly guilty, until I can be sure with moral certainty that no innocent man or woman is facing lethal injection, no one will meet that fate."[3]

THE PROBLEM OF WRONGFUL CONVICTIONS AND CAPITAL PUNISHMENT

There are so many factors that contribute to the conviction of an innocent person, and the recent focus on these cases has revealed numerous flaws in our criminal-justice system that help create an environment in which wrongful convictions can occur. As of November 2019, the Innocence database from the Death Penalty Information Center shows there have been 167 exonerations of prisoners on death row in the United States since 1973. While some may look at these numbers and see a "victory," perhaps even a sign that the system is working to weed out those who should not be on death row, the fact is, the exact opposite is true. Many of these individuals had to fight for years, sometimes decades, to win their freedom against almost-insurmountable odds. Rather than viewing these numbers as a victory for our criminal-justice system, it begs the question, How many were not exonerated in time? It is not a huge intellectual leap to conclude that in the same time span, there have been many whom the system failed, who were ultimately wrongfully executed.

For example, scientific research has revealed there are consistent factors that can be found in cases of wrongful conviction that should be red flags on appeal and post-conviction challenges. Foremost among these factors is the incidence of eyewitness misidentification. In far too many cases where defendants have been exonerated from death row, we have found that the "eyewitness" identification, upon review, was unreliable and faulty. Making this even more insidious and difficult to be rid of is the fact that, all too often, an innocent mistake is made by well-meaning citizens who are only attempting to aid the process. It is a proven fact that cross-cultural identifications are the most unreliable, yet we find them in far too many cases. In addition to eyewitness misidentification, the leading causes of wrongful convictions are:

a. The use of jailhouse informants;
b. The misuse of forensic science;
c. The unavailability of post-conviction DNA testing; and
d. The misconduct by law enforcement and prosecutors.

In case after case of wrongful convictions, there will be found one or more of these factors upon exoneration. It is tragic to have a wrongful conviction in a non–death-penalty case, but in cases of capital punishment, it is unforgiveable.

THE PRESUMPTION OF INNOCENCE AND OTHER CONSTITUTIONAL SAFEGUARDS

The presumption of innocence is a foundational pillar of the United States criminal-justice system. Our "due process" model of criminal justice demands that we safeguard, above all else, each individual's right to due process, even if it means that some *factually* guilty individuals may go free to safeguard these rights.[4] Our Constitution reflects this priority throughout. In fact, the first ten amendments to the Constitution, commonly referred to as the Bill of Rights, is replete with safeguards designed to protect our individual rights. Within these amendments we find, *inter alia*, the right to remain silent, the right to an attorney, the right to confront witnesses who testify against us, the right against self-incrimination, the right to not be tried twice for the same offense, the right to be free from cruel and unusual punishment,[5] and more. But perhaps no right is more fundamental to what we consider a fair administration of justice than the "presumption of innocence," which accompanies each individual who enters our criminal-justice system[6]and which remains with each individual defendant until dismissal or verdict.

The presumption of innocence is not just a mere expression, but a living, breathing principle upon which our concept of justice is based. It requires, theoretically at least, that every person, no matter their station or title, their wealth or lack thereof, be treated the same—as if they are innocent of all charges leveled against them. From the jailer to the judge, this principle must be applied, and any substantive violation of this principle will set the accused free with all pending charges dismissed.[7] From this principle springs the burden of proof born by the prosecution in every criminal proceeding. This burden is of such import that if a prosecutor does not prove an accused's guilt beyond any "reasonable doubt," the accused must be set free. For example, the Fourth Amendment prohibits unreasonable searches and seizures of individuals, their homes, and their property. Any violation of this prohibition engages the exclusionary rule, which exempts "all" evidence wrongfully obtained as "fruit of the poisonous tree,"[8] notwithstanding the fact that the evidence may clearly point to the subject's guilt. What should be clear, therefore, is that the comprehensive constitutional protection of individuals and individual rights are inviolate.

There exists no greater protection from criminal-justice abuses than the fundamental rights enumerated in the Fourth, Fifth, Sixth, Seventh, and Eighth Amendments to the United States Constitution. These begin with the Fourth Amendment, which provides:

> The right of the people to be secure in their persons, houses papers, and Effects, against unreasonable searches and seizures, shall not be violated, And no Warrants shall issue, but upon probable cause, supported by Oath or affirmation, and particularly describing the place to be searched, and the persons or things to be seized.[9]

Individuals are protected from searches unless there is probable cause or waiver.[10] Warrants are required to search person's homes, dwellings, automobiles, and personal possessions (effects), and these warrants must be specific, particular, descriptive, and supported by a sworn statement.[11] Violation of any of these provisions may, and most probably will, summarily lead to the exclusion of any evidence obtained, no matter how relevant or how conclusively it indicates actual guilt.[12]

For example, in *Malloy versus Hogan*,[13] the Supreme Court clarified and further amplified the principle that the accused may stand mute in the face of state accusations, inquiry, or demands to reveal information.[14] In this pre-conviction phase, our system of justice is so protective of each individual's right to the presumption of innocence that we are willing to accept the very real possibility that some factually guilty criminals may go free. It seems logically inconsistent that we place so much emphasis on the protection of pre-conviction innocence and virtually no emphasis on post- conviction innocence.

To further illustrate this point, look at the protections provided in the Fifth amendment. The Fifth Amendment contains substantively vital safeguards that are fundamental to the protection of individuals who enter our criminal-justice system. In pertinent part, the Fifth Amendment provides that:

> No person shall be held to answer for a capital, or otherwise infamous crime, unless on a presentment or indictment of a Grand Jury. . . . Nor shall any person be subject for the same offence to be twice put in jeopardy of life or limb, nor

> shall be compelled in any criminal case to be a witness against himself, nor be deprived of life liberty, or property, without due process of law.[15]

These individual safeguards are specifically designed to protect the innocent who may enter our criminal-justice system to ensure their innocence is not only protected, but ultimately revealed, and allow them a rightful exit from prosecution.

These protections are continued in the Sixth Amendment, which provides in relevant part:

In all criminal prosecutions, the accused shall enjoy the right to a speedy and public trial, by an impartial jury . . . and to be informed of the nature and cause of the accusation; to be confronted with the witnesses against him; to have compulsory process for obtaining witnesses in his favor, and to have the Assistance of Counsel for his defence.[sic][16]

Finally, it is the Eighth Amendment that endeavors to safeguard the individual's right against lengthy pre-conviction incarceration, unwarranted seizure of property, and reasonable post-conviction punishment. The Eighth Amendment provides in entirety:

> Excessive bail shall not be required, nor excessive fines imposed, nor cruel and unusual punishment inflicted.[17]

All these express principles were drafted to protect the rights of each individual involved in our criminal-justice system.

PRE-CONVICTION *PRESUMPTION* OF INNOCENCE AND *POST-CONVICTION* ACTUAL INNOCENCE

Upon review, what should become patently clear is that great pains were taken by the framers of the Constitution to ensure that innocent individuals were afforded ample opportunity to prove their innocence and avoid conviction. Perhaps nothing embodies this principle more than the *presumption of innocence* inherent in our criminal-justice system.

The accused in every criminal case is presumed innocent until proven guilty, and this presumption travels with him as he winds his way through the criminal process. Further, this presumption will not leave him unless it is overcome by compelling evidence that establishes guilt beyond a reasonable doubt.[18] As we all know, the burden of proof lies with the prosecution (or "State," as it is often said), and this burden remains on the shoulders of the State throughout the criminal process, just as evenly as the presumption of innocence hangs like a halo over the head of the accused. As a result, no defendant is required to prove his innocence and may theoretically remain mute in the face of criminal charges while the prosecution attempts to carry its burden.[19] The presumption of innocence is founded on the first principle of justice, and it is intended not to protect the guilty, but to prevent the conviction of the innocent.[20]

This presumption is so sacrosanct that it is a central feature of jury deliberations. In fact, in all criminal cases, before a jury can begin deliberating, they must be instructed that the defendant is presumed innocent of the charges against him, and that the presumption remains with him throughout every stage of the trial and during their deliberations on the verdict, and it is not overcome unless from all the evidence in the case, they are convinced beyond a reasonable doubt that the defendant is guilty.[21] It is clear that our system of justice was intended to ensure that everyone begins with a fair chance to prove their innocence, even at the risk of letting the factually guilty go free. With this principle firmly established, it is abundantly clear that we have the first part of the equation right—in that everyone is entitled to a fair trial—but what about a fair outcome? Isn't this the true goal of justice?

FORM OVER SUBSTANCE, OR PROCEEDINGS VERSUS OUTCOME

The problem with all these safeguards is this: What happens when they fail to protect the innocent? Do we have correspondingly effective safeguards in place post-conviction to protect the convicted who are actually innocent? The rash of recent exonerations and the development of innocence projects around the nation indicates that our system of justice is failing in this very critical stage of the criminal process: post-conviction claims of innocence.

It is clear that having a fair process does not ensure that in the end, we have a fair outcome. The fact is, at the moment a conviction is determined, all the protective presumptions fly out the window, and great effort is expended by the State to "preserve" the conviction, even in the face of overwhelming questions of a defendant's actual guilt.[22] Herein lies the problem.[23]

One of the most common complaints of convicted defendants is the claim of "ineffective assistance of counsel." This claim is based upon the Sixth Amendment right to counsel; in theory, it posits that any defendant in a criminal proceeding must receive the legal assistance of an attorney, and that attorney must be effective in her efforts to represent the defendant.[24] However, the standard for raising this claim places an extremely high burden upon defendants. First, the defendant must prove that the attorney's conduct deprived him of a "substantive or procedural right,"[25] and if a defendant is successful in meeting this burden, he must next demonstrate that the deprivation was so severe that it undermined the entire legal proceedings.[26] It is only then assumed that the ultimate trial result is "unreliable" and not to be trusted.

Another claim that many factually innocent defendants allege is that "new" evidence exists that will prove they are innocent, and therefore, they are requesting a new hearing to present what they consider to be this new evidence. If the presumption of innocence continued throughout every aspect of a criminal case, then every effort would be used to explore this purported new evidence. After all, when new evidence is alleged to exist, and that evidence is also alleged to be exculpatory, shouldn't it be admissible regardless of circumstances? In fact, if we purport to host a system of justice designed to convict the guilty and free the innocent, isn't this the least we should expect?

However, this is not the case. The fact is, a motion for new trial with new evidence as its basis is a very difficult motion to successfully present. In most states, the standard is so high that it is virtually impossible to reach. To illustrate just how difficult this task is, consider the states of Illinois and Texas.

In both states, following a verdict or finding of guilt, a trial court may grant a new trial as long as the motion is written, it is filed within thirty days of the verdict or finding, and it specifies the grounds upon which the motion is based.[27] The purpose of this option is to allow defendants to have their convictions reviewed at the trial-court level, thereby allowing corrections to be made without filing an actual appeal.[28] But look at what happens when the motion for new trial is based on new evidence.

First, the rules specify that the new evidence must:

1. Be of such a conclusive character that it would probably change the result if a retrial occurred; and
2. It must be material to the trial issue and not merely cumulative; and
3. It must have been discovered after the trial was completed; and
4. It must not have been discoverable before trial through the exercise of due diligence.[29]

Notice that none of these standards has anything to do with whether the defendant is factually innocent or not, which is the primary issue on which every criminal proceeding should be focused.

Claims and Causes of Wrongful Convictions

As we have recently seen in countless post- conviction exonerations, there are numerous factors that can contribute to *factually* innocent individuals being found *legally* guilty of crimes they did not, and in many cases, could not have committed. To ignore the very real possibility that convicted individuals found legally guilty may actually be factually innocent is irresponsible at least, and perhaps immoral as well.

For example, some of the leading causes of wrongful convictions have nothing to do with the defendant and everything to do with our system of justice. Consider that some of the leading contributing factors of wrongful convictions such as untrained or unqualified defense lawyers,[30] jailhouse snitches,[31] misconduct by prosecutors and/or judges,[32] false confessions,[33] and the most common factor of all, eyewitness misidentification,[34] are all related to our system of justice. I submit that innocent defendants should not suffer the burdens of a flaw that is correctable in our system of justice. Now add to the foregoing list the fact that individuals charged with crimes have been known to confess on numerous occasions to crimes they did not commit,[35] and there now exist compelling reasons to institute additional safeguards to protect those who have post- conviction claims of innocence.

Claims of Post-Conviction Innocence and the Death Penalty

Perhaps no case illustrates this fact better than the death penalty case of Troy Davis. Troy Davis was convicted of killing an off-duty police officer. The case received international attention when his claims of innocence began to be revealed. His execution was halted three times to allow his technical arguments to proceed. In the Davis case, new evidence was claimed to be in existence that would have proven his innocence; three of his jurors asserted that if they had known about this evidence at the time of the trial, they would have voted differently; and seven eyewitnesses recanted their identification. Despite his claims of innocence, he was never afforded a new trial where these claims could have been examined, and sadly, he was executed on September 21, 2011, without those claims ever being fully explored.[36] Simply put, our system of justice must operate much better than this to protect those individuals with factual claims of innocence.

Recently, case after case of innocent individuals being exonerated has leaked out through the press. There can be no understating the impact of these cases, not just on the exonerees, but also on the criminal-justice system. The public, heretofore disinterested in the outcome of such cases generally, now has taken new interest in the machinations of this form of justice. Governors and legislators also have begun to question the use of the death penalty when claims of innocence seem to abound. Several governors have taken action.

On April 25, 2012, Governor Dan Malloy of Connecticut signed a bill that repealed the death penalty in the state of Connecticut. In doing so, he said, "It is a time for sober reflection, not celebration."[37]

On December 17, 2007, Governor Jon Corzine signed into legislation a bill repealing the death penalty in the state of New Jersey. In doing so, he expressed, "Today New Jersey is truly evolving. I believe society first must determine if its endorsement of violence begets violence and if violence undermines our commitment to the sanctity of life. To these questions I answer yes."[38]

When Governor Bill Richardson of New Mexico signed legislation halting capital punishment in 2009, he said, "Regardless of my personal opinion about the death penalty, I do not have confidence in the criminal justice system as it currently operates to be the final arbiter when it comes to who lives and who dies for their crime." He went on to note that over 130 death-row inmates have been exonerated in the past ten years.[39]

But perhaps the most compelling statement is that of Illinois governor George Ryan. On January 31, 2000, under Governor George Ryan, Illinois became the first state to declare a moratorium on all executions. In doing so, Governor Ryan released this statement:

> How do you prevent another Anthony Porter—another innocent man from paying the ultimate penalty for a crime he or she did not commit? . . . Today I cannot answer that question.[40]

As if to actually answer his own question, however, Governor Ryan went on to say:

> Until I can be sure that everyone sentenced to death in Illinois is truly guilty, until I can be sure with moral certainty that no innocent man or woman is facing lethal injection, no one will meet that fate.[41]

It is critical that we better address claims of innocence to prevent untold harm to innocent defendants, victims, and families.

CONCLUSION

Post-conviction innocence is a reality that our current criminal-justice system has not fully embraced. It makes no logical sense to place the greatest emphasis on freeing the potentially innocent, even at the risk of letting the guilty go free, but to place virtually no value on ensuring that the post-convicted innocent defendant has an equal opportunity to present their claims of innocence. It must be accepted that witnesses lie, eyewitnesses are often mistaken, victims do not always tell the truth, prosecutors hide exculpatory evidence, judges make improper rulings, and ultimately juries do convict the innocent.

If we accept these facts, then we must reprioritize our post-conviction procedures for protecting claims of innocence. We must eliminate the barriers to presenting new evidence when claims of innocence are made, and we must continue to place emphasis on the principle that all innocent men should go free and add that this principle applies whether pre-, or post-conviction.

NOTES

1. See, generally, John Grisham, *An Innocent Man: Murder in a Small Town* (2006).
2. See *Conviction*, released September 9, 2010, by Fox Searchlight Pictures.
3. See Press release, Illinois Government News Network, "Governor Ryan Declares Moratorium on Executions, Will Appoint Commission to Review Capital Punishment System" (January 31, 2000), available at http://www.illinois.gov/PressRelease/PressReleaseListShow.cfm?RecNum=359.
4. David W. Neubauer and Henry F. Fradella, *America's Courts and the Criminal Justice System, 11th ed.* (Belmont, CA: Wadsworth/Cengage, 2012), 19.
5. These constitutional rights are found in the United States Constitution. U.S. Const. Amendments IV, V, VI, and VIII.
6. See Neubauer, supra at 344. See, additionally, *Bell versus Wolfish*, 441 U.S. 520 (1979).
7. See Neubauer, supra at 68. See also *Brown versus Mississippi*, 297 U.S. 278 (1936).
8. For an explanation of the "fruit of the poisonous tree doctrine," see *Wong Sun versus United States*, 371 U.S. 471 (1963).
9. U.S. Const. Amend IV.
10. Individuals may waive their rights verbally, nonverbally, or by leaving items in "plain view" of the searching agent.
11. See Frances P. Bernat and Nicholas Godlove, *Criminal Procedure Law: Police Issues and the Supreme Court* (Burlington, MA: Jones and Bartlett, 2013), 126.
12. This is the embodiment of exclusionary rule, which albeit a constant victim of legal attack, survives as a hallmark of individual rights and the extreme measures taken to preserve these rights.
13. *Malloy versus Hogan*, 378 U.S. 1 (1960).
14. U.S. Const. Amend. V
15. U.S. Const. Amend V.
16. U.S. Const. Amend V.
17. U.S. Const. Amend. VII.
18. *Flynn versus People*, 222 Ill 303, 78 N.E. 617 (1906).
19. *People versus Magnafichi*, 9 Ill 2d 169, 137 NE2d 256 (1956).
20. Robert S. Hunter, *Trial Handbook for Illinois Lawyers: Criminal, 6th ed.* (Rochester, NY: Lawyers Cooperative Publishing Company, 1989); *People versus Weinstein*, 35 Ill 2d 467, 220 N.E.2d 432 (1966).

21. See, for example, Illinois Courts, *Illinois Pattern Jury Instructions: Criminal*, section 2.03, https://www.illinoiscourts.gov.

22. C. Ronald Huff, "Wrongful Conviction in the United States," in C. Ronald Huff and Martin Killias, eds., *Wrongful Conviction: International Perspectives on Miscarriages of Justice* (Philadelphia: Temple University Press, 2008), 59, 65.

23. First, please allow me to acknowledge that claims of innocence are common and rife at every stage of most criminal proceedings, and as a practical matter, the courts would be hopelessly clogged if every issue were relitigated simply because a defendant claimed innocence. This would certainly frustrate the pursuit of justice. However, to ignore claims of innocence or to refuse to thoroughly investigate them, particularly in death-penalty cases, equally flies in the face of justice. One need look no further than the capital case of Troy Davis, executed with substantial claims of innocence that were never fully explored to determine with any legal certainty the veracity of his claims, which is equally wrong.

24. See, e.g., *Miranda versus Arizona*, 384 U.S. 436 (1966); *Powell versus Alabama*, 287 U.S. 45 (1932); *Gideon versus Wainwright* 372 U.S. 33 (1963); *Brewer versus Williams*, 430 U.S. 387 (1977); *Kirby versus Illinois* 406 U.S. 682 (1972).

25. See *Lockhart versus Fretwell*, 506 U.S. 364, 372 (1993).

26. See *Strickland versus Washington*, 466 U.S. 668, 687 (1984).

27. Section 725 ILCS 5/116-1 (a), (b), and (c) (2010). Retrieved from Illinois General Assembly compiled statutes.

28. See, for example, *People versus Pierce*, 35 Ill. Dec. 925, 80 Ill. App. 3d 514, 400 N.E.2d 62 (1980).

29. This standard for a new trial is the model for most motions for new trials. See, for example, Texas Code of Criminal Procedure, Article 40.001, which mirrors the Illinois and Florida criminal codes.

30. Innocence Project, Bad Lawyering, available at_http://www.innocenceproject.org/understand/Bad-Lawyering.php (last visited July 13, 2013).

31. Innocence Project, Informants/Snitches, available at http://www.innocenceproject.org/understand/Snitches-Informants.php (last visited August 31, 2013).

32. Innocence Project, Government Misconduct, available at http://www.innocenceproject.org/understand/Government-Misconduct.php (last visited August 4, 2013).

33. Saul M. Kassin, "False Confessions: Causes, Consequences, and Implications for Reform," *Current Directions in Psychological Science* 17: (2008), 248–49.

34. Innocence Project, Eyewitness Misidentification, available at http://www.innocence project.org/understand/Eyewitness-Misidentification.php (last visited September 12, 2013).

35. It is troubling to accept that innocent individuals routinely admit to guilt. Often this can be based upon misinformation, a belief that they are in no position financially or otherwise to continue to assert their claims of innocence, and from the wearing down from law-enforcement abuse both psychologically and, to a lesser extent, physically. See, generally, http://www.innocenceproject.org/False-Confessions.php.

36. Death Penalty Information Center, "Troy Davis Facing Execution in Georgia Despite Recantation of Eyewitnesses" (2008; 2011), available at http://www.deathpenaltyinfo.org/documents/2008.pdf.

37. Bernie Davidow, "Without Fanfare, Malloy Signs Bill Abolishing Death Penalty," *Hartford Courant*, April 25, 2012, http://courantblogs.com/capitol-watch/without-fanfare-malloy-signs-bill-abolishing-death-penalty/.

38. Ibid.

39. Press release, Governor Bill Richardson, "Governor Bill Richardson Signs Repeal of the Death Penalty" (March 18, 2009), available at http://www.deathpenaltyinfo.org/document/richardsonstatement.pdf.

40. Press release, Illinois Government News Network, "Governor Ryan Declares Moratorium on Executions, Will Appoint Commission to Review Capital Punishment System" (January 31, 2000), available at http://www.illinois.gov/PressReleases/PressReleasesListShow.cfm?RecNum=359.

41. Ibid.

Chapter 9

Life Without Parole: The Alternative to Capital Punishment

Proponents of capital punishment often argue that the death penalty provides several vital functions to a safe and cohesive society governed by the rule of law. Among these benefits, they posit, is the fact that a death-penalty defendant, once executed, cannot be a threat to the public again. This is certainly true, but is it the best or only means of eliminating this type of threat? Is it worth the cost associated with removing the threat? Are we becoming—as a society—a little more brutal with each successive execution, and does this brutality seep into other areas of our daily lives? What happens to a society that becomes desensitized not only to death, but also to cause the death of others? Can the rise in school shootings, a very uniquely American phenomenon, be somehow related to this desensitization to death and the perpetration of death? Has the rise in violence in our major cities—like Chicago, a city so plagued with gun violence and murders that the news of a deadly shooting, in broad daylight, has become a normal occurrence—become a symptom of a criminal-justice system that embraces violence in its ultimate sanction? It is the task of social scientists to answer these questions and draw conclusory analysis, but it certainly could be argued that we are seeing the byproducts of a culture too enamored with deadly violence.

I would not point out all the myriad problems associated with violence with capital punishment without offering alternatives to the sanction. As we have seen, there is simply no good method of execution, so why do it at all? Court-sanctioned executions are too costly and too inhumane, and with the very real risk of executing the innocent, there must be a better alternative. Fortunately, there is. The alternative recommended is life without the possibility of parole (LWOP)

One of the first and most obvious benefits of LWOP is that we completely eliminate the possibility of executing an innocent person. This is no small benefit. Our criminal-justice system exists to mete out justice, not to create an even greater injustice by executing the innocent. By using LWOP as an alternative, we completely eliminate this possibility and leave open the opportunity to correct a wrongful conviction of a death-row inmate, of which we have seen many examples in this book.

DEATH IN PRISON IS CERTAIN WITH LWOP

The intent underlying the sentence of life without the possibility of parole is that those who have been sentenced to this punishment are intended to die in prison. This has been, and continues to be, a goal *inter alia* of LWOP, to provide this type of certainty. Is it possible that someone who has received this sentence to be paroled, pardoned, or exonerated? Yes, but if this were to occur, there would have to be legal justification for doing so, such as advancements in technology proving innocence, and this legal justification would actually be a positive outcome for our criminal-justice system. Beyond this, however, those sentenced to life in prison are expected to actually die in prison.

VICTIMS AND THEIR FAMILIES PREFER THE FINALITY OF LWOP

Those who are sentenced to die by execution are granted automatic appeals and court-appointed lawyers when the defendant is unable to afford one (virtually every defendant falls into this category). The average length of time spent on death row with appeals pending is over seventeen years. With each successive appeal, there is the possibility of the conviction being overturned, or a new trial ordered, or the sentence reduced. Victims and their families are forced to ride this legal roller coaster with every step of each appeal and relive what, for most, is their greatest pain. The length of the appellate process for those sentenced to be executed simply prolongs the pain of the victims and their families. However, with LWOP, no special appellate consideration is given, which limits the number of appeals and thereby limits the possibility of a reduction or a reversal of the sentence. Victims and their families prefer this finality, which allows them to move on from what is usually a horrible event.

DEATH IN PRISON IS A VERY HARSH SENTENCE

There are some who would argue that those individuals sentenced to be executed should not be afforded the luxury of living out their lives in prison, but the harsh reality is that living and dying in prison provides few luxuries and is a very unpleasant way to live out the remainder of one's life. Most prisons are overcrowded, dangerous places with inadequate health care and few programs for the incarcerated. This is a particularly unpleasant way to spend a few years, but to live in these conditions for often thirty or forty years—with no hope of release—has to be a very horrible existence. LWOP prisoners are given no special treatment, are often exempt from rehabilitation programs, are housed in high-security facilities with corresponding high-security measures imposed at every turn, are often housed in crowded group cells, and are afforded very few privileges. The irony is that those on death row are usually in more comfortable, single-person cells, have hope that their sentences will be reduced or reversed, and often are elevated to international celebrity status while their appeals wind their way through the criminal justice system.[1] Their names are associated with legal precedent, Supreme Court cases hear their facts and arguments, and in the end, they may have their death sentences overturned.

LWOP SAVES THE TAXPAYERS MONEY

Housing prisoners on death row is expensive. There are additional security personnel and procedures, there are special housing requirements, and there is generally a great deal of oversight for the conduct and conditions on death row. Death-row defendants are not only expensive to house and maintain, but they also require much more expensive legal representation at every turn. For example, in California, it has cost taxpayers an additional ninety million dollars per year to house their death-row inmates, and between the years 1977 and 2002, California taxpayers spent 250 million dollars to ultimately execute just eleven death-row inmates.[2]

LWOP PROTECTS AGAINST WRONGFUL EXECUTIONS

Since 1973, 153 individuals have been exonerated from death row, often at the very last minute. Others have not been so fortunate. LWOP is the great legal safety net that allows us to correct any mistakes we may have made in convicting the innocent. Our system of justice was designed to punish the guilty and protect the innocent. This should be true even for those charged and convicted of death-eligible crimes. LWOP provides us with time to review every legitimate claim of innocence and to do so before an irreversible sanction has been imposed. In my view, this is the single most compelling reason for replacing capital punishment with life without the possibility of parole.

Death-penalty advocates are generally troubled with LWOP as an option. It is argued that by not executing some of the admittedly worst offenders, we continue to allow them to be a threat to the public, either at large, if they should escape, or to the prison personnel and prison population should they remain incarcerated for life. While these are valid concerns and deserve serious consideration, the fact is, prison escapes are rare, and rarer still are they successful in creating long-term freedom for the escapee(s). Are we going to continue a sentencing sanction rife with practical and humane problems on the predicate that a prisoner *may* escape someday or harm those with whom they are imprisoned? Joseph Ingle, a minister to death-row offenders and an opponent of LWOP, believes this option suffers from the same malady as the death penalty in that LWOP, just like the death penalty, "gives up" on the offender, painting them as hopeless and beyond redemption. Henry Schwarzschild, former ACLU director of the Capital Punishment Project, agrees with Ingle and calls LWOP "mindless," "humanly and economically wasteful," and "morally repellant in its very assumptions."[3]

There is another version of LWOP that goes even further in eliminating the dangers of capital punishment while also providing a means of achieving another highly valued sentencing goal, and that is rehabilitation. This alternative is life without the *probability* of parole. This phrase can be attributed to the late professor Hugo Bedau, professor of philosophy at Tufts University and a staunch advocate for ending capital punishment. Critics of both capital punishment and LWOP have argued that both alternatives essentially discard the individual and consider them beyond hope or redemption. As Professor Bedau has stated, "Both penalties amount to human garbage disposal."[4]

Table 9.1. Death-Penalty States Offering Life without Parole (LWOP)

Alabama	*Louisiana*	*South Carolina*
Arizona	Missouri	Tennessee
Arkansas	Montana	Texas
California	Nevada	Utah
Florida	North Carolina	Wyoming
Georgia	Ohio	-PLUS-
Idaho	Oklahoma	By Federal Statute
Indiana	Oregon	By Military Statute
Kansas	Pennsylvania	
Kentucky	South Carolina	
Mississippi	South Dakota	

Source: Death Penalty Information Center (DPIC), Sentencing Alternatives: Life Without Parole, deathpenaltyinfo.org, last retrieved August 3, 2023.

WHAT SHOULD CAPITAL JURIES BE TOLD ABOUT LWOP?

Is it a denial of rights to a capital defendant not to have his jury informed about the sentencing alternative of life without parole? There is ample research available to suggest that jurors are often mistaken about the results of a life sentence and that they operate from this base of misperception. If the jurors believe that a life sentence is not actually a long sentence and that a defendant sentenced to life may be released in a relatively short period of time, this mistaken belief could cause a jury to lean more toward a death sentence rather than a life sentence, which would be significantly unfair to the death defendant. Juries do consider future dangers to the public or others, and this concern undoubtedly will impact their decisions. The Supreme Court tackled this issue in *Simmons versus South Carolina*,[5] and the court's answer was that if the future danger from the defendant has been made an issue in the capital trial, then the jury must be informed that LWOP is the alternative to a death sentence, rather than simply a life sentence. Evan Mandery, in *Capital Punishment in America*, provides an excellent summary of *Simmons*:

> In *Simmons*, the prosecution argued that Simmons's future dangerousness was a factor for the jury to consider in deciding the appropriate punishment. Simmons requested an instruction informing the jury that life imprisonment did not include parole eligibility in his case. During deliberations, the jury sent a question to the judge asking whether the defendant would be parole-eligible. The Court held that on these facts, due process required that the defendant be entitled to inform the jury of his parole eligibility.[6]

The *Simmons* Court was not the only Court to weigh in on this topic; in *California versus Ramos*, the Court upheld the constitutionality of the requirement that jurors be informed about the governor's power to commute sentences, and in *Ramdass versus Angelone*, the Court ruled that state judges are not required to give an LWOP instruction if they find "that a defendant given that sentence may at some point become eligible for parole." Finally, in *Brown versus Texas*, the Court rejected the notion that jurors are required to be informed of the possibility of lengthy minimum sentences in those states that do not have LWOP as a possible alternative to a death sentence.[7]

Whether we have as an option life without the *possibility* of parole or without the *probability* of parole, we accomplish several major goals by substituting the sentence of death with LWOP, not the least of which is negating the possibility of executing an innocent defendant. In fact, every primary goal that the death penalty accomplishes is likewise accomplished with LWOP: society is protected from future crimes by the defendant, punishment is meted out in a large quantity commensurate with the crime of which the capital defendant has been convicted, and the cost of housing the capital defendant for life is drastically reduced from the cost of administering the death sentence with its attendant delays, appellate costs, and death-row obligations.

Finally, it is arguable that no Eighth Amendment violations of the "cruel and unusual punishment" clause will result from a sentence of life without the possibility of parole. After all is said and done, we no longer need the sanction of capital punishment in our system of criminal justice; it is time for this form of punishment to end in the United States.

NOTES

1. See, for example, the case of Troy Davis, executed in Jackson, Georgia, in 2011, after having been found guilty of the murder of a police officer. His case gained international prominence for his compelling claims of actual innocence, and it remains one of the cases in which an innocent man was likely executed.

2. In 2019, California governor Gavin Newsome declared a moratorium on further executions in California, although the death penalty is technically still a legal penal sanction. In declaring this moratorium, Governor Newsom referenced the high cost to taxpayers and the prospects of executing an innocent person. See Scott Martelle, "California halted executions, now it should abolish the death penalty," *Los Angeles Times*, December 3, 2021.

3. Ibid., or see *Death Quest III*, 205.

4. Ibid.

5. See *Simmons versus South Carolina*, 512 U.S. 154 (1994).

6. See Evan J. Mandery, *Capital Punishment in America: A Balanced Examination*, 2nd ed. (Sudbury, MA: Jones and Bartlett, 2012), 404.

7. Ibid., 404.

Chapter 10

Final Considerations

Capital Punishment

The issue of whether to punish citizens who commit the most serious crimes with capital punishment has been debated since its inception in this country, and this debate is not likely to end anytime soon. In writing this book, my intent was not to disparage those who have legitimately held beliefs in the value of maintaining the ultimate sanction. To be sure, it is understood that capital punishment rests upon the very simple proposition that more punishment is appropriate for more crime, and the most severe punishment is appropriate for the most severe crimes. This simple proposition extends from two equally simple theories: the biblical "eye for an eye" form of deterrent, and that the experience of witnessing, or learning of, a capital execution will serve to deter others. The problem is, there is no conclusive evidence that capital punishment actually deters people from committing capital crimes; in fact, I would argue that capital crimes, by the very nature of their severity, fall into the category of undeterrable crimes. If this is, in fact, true, we must take a serious look at capital punishment as a penal sanction and the effect it is having, and has had, and ask ourselves, isn't it time to acknowledge that this sanction, for a whole host of reasons, is ineffective.

As we take a moment to consider the future implications of continuing to have a death penalty in America, there are a few final areas that need to be addressed. Some of the fundamental questions we need to ask ourselves as an enlightened nation are: How are we going to treat the mentally ill who have committed capital offenses? Do we approach them the same as if they were not mentally impaired? What about the poor? Should our legal system continue to execute the indigent when research has shown repeatedly that the rich do not get executed and the poor do? What about the young?[1] *Roper versus Simmons*[2] outlawed the execution of teenagers under the age of eighteen, but science tells us that mental development is incomplete for those who are eighteen to twenty-five years old. Should the same standard apply to this age group? Lastly, what does having capital punishment do to a society? Does the brutalization of execution seep past the confines of our prisons and enter the mainstream of society, causing even more brutalization? These are all considerations worthy of deeper exploration.

THE EXECUTION OF JUVENILE OFFENDERS

The barbaric practice of executing juveniles was finally outlawed by the United States Supreme Court in 2005 with the ruling in *Roper versus Simmons*,[3] but the debate of whether to execute juveniles has raged on ever since. For example, Michael Brim argues in a *Denver University Law Review* article that "the court should not have drawn a bright line rule at the arbitrary age of eighteen because age does not define one's character, judgment, maturity, personal responsibility, or moral guilt."[4] While Joseph Hoffman questioned whether a ban on the death penalty for juveniles is consistent with the fundamental retributive goal of ensuring that every person who commits a crime receives his or her just deserts, or the punishment that is appropriate in light of the harm caused by the crime and the offender's culpability.[5] These arguments and questions represent so many others who assert similar, if not identical arguments in favor of continuing capital punishment for juvenile offenders. Both lines of legal reasoning are flawed and miss the fundamental point, which is: juveniles are underdeveloped, and we, as a society, have chosen to recognize this lack of development in every area of society, except in the area where it matters most: our criminal-justice system.

It has long been established that juveniles are not mature, that their moral development is lacking, that their ability to reason is flawed, and that their decision-making ability and appreciation of the consequences of their decisions is not fully formed. We have come to accept this in numerous other areas of our everyday lives. We do not allow juveniles to purchase cigarettes; we do not allow juveniles to purchase alcohol; we do not allow juveniles to join the military; we do not allow juveniles under the age of sixteen even to hold a job without a work permit signed by a responsible adult—and the list of juvenile restrictions can go on and on in many other areas of everyday life. But perhaps the most telling is the fact that insurance companies charge more to insure juvenile drivers—for the very same reasons that we should not hold them completely and singularly responsible for their acts, no matter how heinous. These billion-dollar companies understand that juveniles are not fully developed and are likely to make poor choices while driving that can lead to otherwise-avoidable accidents. If insurance companies can recognize this fact, why, then, can't our criminal-justice system?

But wait—it *does* recognize that juveniles are different. In fact, our criminal-justice system has created a completely different court system to handle juvenile cases, called the Juvenile Court System, whose entire purpose is to correct and rehabilitate underage offenders. This system does not even allow findings of guilt, but rather, it ends proceedings with determinations such as "deeming a juvenile in need of supervision," making them "wards of the court," or, in the theoretically most severe cases, incarcerating them in juvenile facilities for their correction. Proceedings in these cases are closed to the public, have restricted publication, and protect the identities of juveniles in the system. Great effort is made to protect juvenile offenders and to provide them with direction, supervision, intervention, and support so they can have the best chance at rehabilitation in light of their underdevelopment.

With all this as a backdrop, why, then, is it that we throw all this logic and reasoning out of the window when a juvenile commits a heinous act? Is it at this point that the controlling factor becomes the severity of the act? Does the act itself change the age of the offender? Does the act infuse increased levels of maturity and development, so that now, by merely acting, we can impute increased development to the juvenile offender? Clearly, this is ridiculous logic and is not supported by science or reason. Juveniles should never have been subjected to capital punishment, and they never again should be.

Those who are mentally and morally underdeveloped due to a lack of age and experience should never have this factor ignored when it comes to assessing their culpability. The Supreme Court got it right with *Roper v. Simmons*, and I would like to see the age extended far beyond the current restriction of under eighteen. The death penalty should be abolished, and the juvenile death penalty—i.e., for those over the age of eighteen—should be the first to go.

EXECUTION OF THE MENTALLY ILL

There is a recurring theme that can readily be found among almost any collection of death-row inmates. To be certain, they are there because they have been accused and convicted of a very serious criminal act; it is also likely they were not represented by a first-rate attorney throughout the course of their trial and ultimate conviction; so, too, is it likely that they come from a lower socioeconomic status, which placed them in societal positions in which none of us would want to find ourselves. All these factors are likely to be found in ample supply among death-row inmates, but they are not the factors I point to at this juncture. The factor I point to, by its mere existence among those condemned to execution, begs the question, Who are we? Who are we as a society? Who are we as a civilized group of people? Who are we as advocates for truth, justice, and equality for all? The factor I am pointing to is our continued execution of the mentally ill.

Every law student and lawyer has been drilled during their criminal law courses in law school that two things must exist for a "crime" to emerge: 1) a guilty act, or *actus reus*, and 2) a guilty mind, or *mens rea*. It is the *mens rea*, or guilty mind, on which I would like to focus: the requirement that someone knowingly and with mental understanding decides to commit a criminal act. The question then becomes, how much understanding are we willing to attribute to the criminal defendant who does not meet the IQ level of being excused from their acts by reason of insanity, but who clearly suffers from mental retardation or illness, and that retardation or illness did not allow them to make a reasonable decision or properly calculate the consequences of the decision they made? Here are some of the mentally ill people whom we, as a nation, have executed:

Andrew Brannon, a Vietnam War veteran, sixty-six years old with no prior criminal record, disabled with PTSD and bipolar disorder. Executed in Georgia on January 13, 2015.

Cecil Clayton, seventy-four years old, suffered from dementia, had an IQ of seventy-one, and was missing a significant part of his brain due to an accident. Executed in Missouri on March 17, 2015.

Gary Allen, diagnosed with schizophrenia and dementia caused by seizures and drug addiction. Executed in Oklahoma on November 11, 2012.

Robert Moorman, mentally disabled and sexually abused throughout his childhood and into adulthood. Executed in Arizona on February 29, 2012.[6]

This is by no means an exhaustive list; there are many, many seriously mentally ill persons whom our criminal-justice system has chosen to make no exception for, and they were executed for crimes that can be directly traced to their mental illness. The question we must ask is this: For the mentally ill, or those suffering from severe intellectual disabilities, shouldn't we hold them to a lesser standard of culpability when we know their brain function and ability to reason is impaired?

I submit that we should. I further submit, in support of this argument, it is no accident that so many of the criminally mentally impaired end up on death row. The fact is, if not for their mental impairment, they would have made different choices along the way that would likely have prevented them from landing in a place that the crimes they committed warrant them being charged with a death-eligible offense. Had they had the ability to reason normally, they would not have chosen to commit the crime because the normal ability to reason would have informed them the act was wrong, or at the very least, that committing such an act would not be worth the potential consequences that flow from that act. It does not take an intellectual leap of Olympic proportions to see the logic in this position. However, there are those who would vehemently disagree.

For example, Barry Latzer, in his article "Misplaced Compassion: The Mentally Retarded and the Death Penalty,"[7] argues that it is "inappropriate to make the assumption that retardation handicaps one to the point at which ordinary criminal punishment becomes inhumane." He further argues that "it is not inhumane to impose on morally responsible people constitutionally acceptable punishments that 'fit' their crimes." To be sure, Barry Latzer is a widely respected professor, scholar, criminologist, and lawyer, and the opinions he expresses encompass many of the similar opinions of those who support capital punishment. Respectfully, however, here is where Latzer and those who have similar beliefs are wrong: If we are going to have a requirement that mental state is a fundamental ingredient before an action may be considered a crime, and if we are going to recognize that children are, as a matter of science and law, unable to form the requisite mental state, then by definition any factor that reduces a person's mental ability to that of an underage child must place that person in the same category as that of a child. This is true whether the "child" is five or fifty-five. It is the mental ability that we first consider, not the act, no matter how heinous, egregious, or reprehensible. Further, we are not arguing that these individuals should escape total responsibility for their actions; we are simply stating what should be obvious, that it is wrong and inhumane to execute anyone who is so afflicted.

Finally, one of the primary goals of those in favor of capital punishment is deterrence of others. This, too, falls flat when applied to the mentally retarded. The mentally ill cannot appreciate their actions in a sufficient enough degree to deter themselves from action, and it is illogical to believe that another similarly situated mentally ill person would see the execution and thereby be deterred. We have other means of deterring criminals and protecting society from those who are dangerous, and even mentally ill dangerous offenders can be incapacitated without executing them. We are better than this.

CAPITAL PUNISHMENT UNFAIRLY TARGETS THE POOR

Should poverty be a significant factor in sentencing? Should a judge, when sentencing a person convicted of a capital crime, look at the facts of the crime, the criminal history of the defendant, the likelihood of repeat offenses, and the defendant's level of poverty? All the foregoing should be considered, but poverty, absolutely not! Within our system of justice, specifically when it comes to sentencing, we do not ask, what does poverty have to do with the severity of a sentence? The answer should always be "nothing at all," but the reality is far more different and disturbing.

The fact is, death row is populated with some of the poorest defendants in our criminal-justice system. They have been represented by some of the worst capital defense lawyers in our system of justice, and those lawyers have been appointed or assigned to represent these defendants for one reason and one reason only—they cannot afford to hire counsel on their own. They cannot afford better-skilled, better-trained, and better-financed lawyers, which, in all probability, would have most certainly prevented them from ever arriving on death row. Is this a fair administration of justice? Should we be content to allow inmate after inmate to be executed, knowing that they were not adequately represented? Shouldn't we insist upon the absolute best level of representation when the harshest penalty in our array of punishments is at stake? Renowned death-penalty lawyer Stephen Bright, in his article "Counsel for the Poor: The Death Sentence Not for the Worst Crime but for the Worst Lawyer," stated:

> The process of sorting out who is most deserving of society's ultimate punishment does not work when the most fundamental component of the adversary system, competent representation by counsel, is missing.[8]

Or, as Bryan Stevenson so aptly stated, capital punishment really means: "*them without the capital get the punishment.*"[9] This is such a significant factor because in all criminal defenses, the skill and resources of the attorney will positively affect the ultimate outcome of the case being presented. Being able to provide persuasive testimony, expert witnesses, and jury consultants, and being adept at weaving facts and science together to tell a favorable story, is absolutely critical to the defendant's outcome, and this is routinely found with the best attorneys and rarely found with the worst. The best attorneys, as it is with most things, are expensive.

So, then, what is the answer? Surely we cannot expect the state to spend taxpayer dollars to pay the exorbitant prices of presenting the best defenses? To that I would reply, either we are willing to level the playing field when it comes to capital representation and match the resource capabilities that the state has to prosecute, or we stop executing those who cannot afford the best representation.

WHAT DOES CONTINUING THE PRACTICE OF CAPITAL PUNISHMENT SAY ABOUT US AS A NATION?

What does our practice of capital punishment say about us as a society? Are we not enlightened enough to the point that we can see the inherent injustices surrounding this practice? What has been the downfall of the great civilizations of past history? Hasn't the fall come from an implosion within? It does not take much of a search to see that the fall of the great Roman empire came from the fraying of the fabric of their society within. The Mayans, the Incas, the Egyptians, the North American Indigenous people, the USSR—all can attribute as a leading factor internal strife as a cause of their downfall.

Russian writer and philosopher Fyodor Dostoevsky once said, "You can judge a society by how well it treats its prisoners." Mahatma Gandhi once said, "I cannot in all conscience agree to anyone being sent to the gallows." Martin Luther King Jr., who was greatly influenced by Gandhi, said, "an eye for an eye leaves everyone blind."

Mother Teresa, a canonized saint, was also vehemently opposed to capital punishment throughout her lifetime of service. For Mother Teresa, capital punishment violated the sacredness of life, an ethic she believed must be applied whether that life was preborn or on death row. For her, this was a simple, uncomplicated position to take, that all life was sacred and should be preserved. As to a person accused of a crime, she once implored the governor of California on behalf of a condemned man scheduled to be executed, "Do what Jesus would do and forgive him." She was not alone. Dr. Benjamin Rush,[10] one of the early opponents of capital punishment, also did not believe executions held any deterrent value. He did not believe executions dissuaded people from committing crimes they had already contemplated committing; in fact, he was one of the first to believe that capital punishment increased crime, and he was one of the first to recognize the potential harm to society that this sanction could cause, pointing out that the mere existence of the death penalty had a brutalizing effect on the general populace. Perhaps Cesare Beccaria said it best:

> It seems to me absurd that the laws, which are an expression of the public will, which detest and punish homicide, should themselves commit it, and that to deter citizens from murder, they order a public one.[11]

Beccaria's words are profound and underscore the absurdity of capital punishment in a modern age.

The time has come to abolish capital punishment in America. I sincerely hope you agree.

NOTES

1. Charles Scott, "*Roper v. Simmons*: Can Juvenile Offenders Be Executed?" *Journal of American Academy of Psychiatry and the Law* (2005), Jaapl.org.

2. *Roper versus Simmons*, 543 U.S. 551 (2005).

3. *Roper versus Simmons*, 543 U.S. 551 (2005).

4. Michael Brim, "A Sneak Preview into How the Court Took Away a State's Right to Execute Sixteen- and Seventeen-Year-Old Juveniles: The Threat of Execution Will No Longer Save an Innocent Victim's Life," *Denver University Law Review*, 82: (2005), 739.

5. Joseph Hoffman, "The Perils of Line-Drawing: Juveniles and the Death Penalty," *Hastings Law Journal*, 40: (1988–1989), 229.

6. DPIC, "Mentally Ill Prisoners Who Were Executed," deathpenaltyinfo.org/policy-issues-mental-illness-/mentally-ill-prisoners-who-were-executed.

7. Barry Latzer, "Misplaced Compassion: The Mentally Retarded and the Death Penalty," *Criminal Law Bulletin* 38: (2002), 327.

8. Stephen Bright, "Counsel for the Poor: The Death Sentence Not for the Worst Crime but for the Worst Lawyer," *Yale Law Journal*, 103: (1994), 1835, 1837.

9. Bryan Stevenson, cited in *Death Quest*, Robert Bohm, ed. (Andersen Publishing, 2007), 306.

10. Dr. Benjamin Rush (1747–1813) was a Philadelphia physician, singer, and an original signatory of the Declaration of Independence. He founded the Philadelphia Society for Alleviating the Miseries of Public Prisons, one of the first groups to organize against capital punishment. See Robert M. Bohm, *Death Quest III*, 5–6.

11. Cesare Beccaria, as quoted in Robert M. Bohm, *Death Quest III*, 192.

Bibliography

Acker, James R., and Allison D. Redlich. (2011). *Wrongful Convictions: Law Science and Policy*, Carolina Academic Press.

Alarcon, Arthur, and Paula Mitchell. (2012). "Costs of Capital Punishment in California: Will voters choose reform this November?" *Loyola of Los Angeles Law Review*, 46, S1–S35.

Alarcon, Arthur L., Paula M. Mitchell. (2011). *Executing the Will of the Voters? A Roadmap to mend or end the California's Legislature's Multi-Billion-dollar Death Penalty Debacle*, 44 LOY. LA. L. REV. S41 (2011).

Amnesty International, *Recent Cost Studies*, https://www.amnestyusa.org/issues/death-penalty/death-penalty-facts/death-penalty-cost/ (retrieved March 24, 2020).

Armour, Marilyn Peterson, Mark S. Umbreit. (2002). "Assessing the Impact of the Ultimate Penal Sanction on Homicide Survivors: A Two State Comparison," 96 *Marquette L. Rev.* 1(2002).

Armstrong, Ken, Steve Mills. (1999). "Inept Defenses Cloud Verdict," *Chicago Tribune*, November 15, 1999.

Banner, Stuart. (2002). *The Death Penalty: An American History*. Cambridge, Mass.: Harvard University Press.

Baumgartner, Frank R., Suzanna L. DeBoef, Amber E. Boydstun. (2008). *The Decline of the Death Penalty and the Discovery of Innocence.* New York: Cambridge University Press.

Bellivier, Florence. (2017). *The Death Penalty: A Punishment for the Poor?* FIDH International Federation for Human Rights, October 10, 2017, www.FIDH.org (retrieved March 1, 2021).

Bernat, Frances P., Nicholas Godlove. (2013). *Criminal Procedure Law: Police Issues and the Supreme Court.* Burlington, MA: Jones & Bartlett), 126.

Blackstone, Sir William. (1765). *Commentaries on the Laws of England.* Oxford: Oxford University Press, Wilford Prest, ed. (2016).

Bohm, Robert M. (2013). *Capital Punishment's Collateral Damage*. Durham, NC: Carolina Academic Press.

Bohm, Robert M. (2007). *Death Quest III: An Introduction to the Theory and Practice of Capital Punishment in the United States*. Boston: Anderson Publishing.

Borchard, Edwin M. (1932). *Convicting the Innocent: Sixty-Five Actual Errors of Criminal Justice.* Garden City Publishing Company.

Bright, Stephen B. (1999). *Neither Equal or Just: The Rationing and Denial of Legal Services to the Poor When Life and Liberty Are at Stake*. New York University School of Law, Annual Survey of American Law, 1997, 1–53.

Bright, Stephen. (1999). "Counsel for the Poor: The Death Sentence: Not for the Worst Crime but for the Worst Lawyer," 103 *Yale Law Journal* 1835 (May 1994).

Bright, Stephen B. (2016). "The Punishment for Having a Bad Lawyer Shouldn't Be the Death Penalty." *Guardian*, www.theguardian.org, October 4, 2016, retrieved March 7, 2021. New York University School of Law Annual Survey of American Law, 1997, 1–53.

Cueto, Emma. (2019). *Death Row Cases Stirs Fears over Quality of Defense Counsel*, Law 360 May 5, 2019, retrieved March 3, 2021, www.law360.com.

Darah Gregorian, Haley Talbot, NBCnews.com, March 18, 2021, "'*Get a Tall Oak Tree': Rep. Chip Roy of Texas Defends Apparent Pro-Lynching Remarks.*" https://www.NBCnews.com, retrieved March 20, 2021.

Darrow, Clarence. (1928). *The Futility of the Death Penalty: Capital Punishment Is No Deterrent to Crime.* The Forum, reprinted in Clarence Darrow, *Verdicts Out of Court*. (1963). Chicago: Elephant Paperback Publishing.

Davidow, Bernie. (2012). "Without Fanfare, Malloy Signs Bill Abolishing Death Penalty." *Hartford Courant*, April 25, 2012, http://courantblogs.com/capitol-watch/without-fanfare-malloy-signs-bill-abolishing-death-penalty/.

Dieter, Richard C., *What Politicians Don't Say about the High Cost of the Death Penalty*, Death Penalty Information Center, 1994.

DPIC (Death Penalty Information Center), Facts & Research: *The History of the Death Penalty*, retrieved on March 1, 2021. http://www.deathpenaltyinfo.org.

DPIC (Death Penalty Information Center), *Death Penalty Representation*, retrieved March 1, 2021. http://www.deathpenaltyinfo.org/policy-issues/death-penalty-representation/articles-regarding-capital-reprsentation.

DPIC (Death Penalty Information Center), *Articles Regarding Capital Representation*, citing the *Dallas Morning News*, November 10, 2000. http://www.deathpenaltyinfo.org, retrieved March 1, 2021.

DPIC (Death Penalty Information Center), "Why Is Texas #1 in Executions?" https://www.dpic.org, *Journal of Criminal Law and Criminology*, 881 (1) 242–302.

DPIC, Death Penalty Information Center, *Report of the Judicial Council Death Penalty Advisory Committee 1* (February 13, 2014), http://deathpenaltyinfo.org/documets/KSCost2014.pdf.

DPIC, Death Penalty Information Center, citing the Maryland Commission on Capital Punishment, https://deathpenaltyinfo.org/stories/Maryland-commission-on-capital-punishment, retrieved March 26, 2020.

DPIC, The Death Penalty Information Center, *Executions by State and Year*. https://www.deathhpenaltyinfo.org, retrieved March 20, 2020.

Dripps, D. (1998). *Ineffective Assistance of Counsel: The Case for an Ex-Ante Parity Standard.* Equal Justice USA, Poverty and Poor Legal Defense, Equal Justice USA, www.ejusa.org, retrieved March 7, 2021.

Equal Justice USA. *Justice for a Few? A Punishment for the Poor*. Equal Justice USA, http://www.ejusa.org, retrieved February 19, 2021.

Equal Justice, USA. *About the Death Penalty: Inadequate Counsel: The Death Penalty Is Mostly Imposed on Poor People Who Cannot Afford to Hire an Effective Lawyer*. Equal Justice Initiative, http://www.eji.org, retrieved March 3, 2021.

Erickson, David. (1993). Death Penalty Focus of Cal., "Capital Punishment at What Price: An Analysis of the Cost Issue in A Strategy to Abolish the Death Penalty" 25 (Spring 1993).

Fellner, James, Sarah Tofte. (2006). *So Long as They Die: Lethal Injection in the United States*. Human Rights Watch (April 2006).

Findley, Keith A., and Michael Scott. "The Multiple Dimensions of Tunnel Visions in Criminal Cases," *Wisconsin Law Review*, 2006.

Gould, Jon B., and Richard A Leo. "One Hundred Years Later: Wrongful Convictions After a Century of Research," *Journal of Criminal Law & Criminology*, 2010.

Graczyk, Michael. (2016). "Texas Lawyer Who Lost All Death Penalty Cases Says He's Done." *Denver Post*, August 14, 2016, retrieved March 4, 2021, www .denverpost.com.

Grann, David. "Trial by Fire: Did Texas Execute an Innocent Man?" *New Yorker*, September 2009.

Gray, Pamela, Richard LaGravenese, writers. (2010). *Conviction*, Tony Goldwyn, director, Fox Searchlight Pictures, release date: September 11, 2010.

Gregorian, Darah. (2021). "*Get a Tall Oak Tree*," NBC News, http://nbcnews.com, quoting Representative Chip Roy of Texas, retrieved March 20, 2021.

Grisham, John. (2006). *The Innocent Man: Murder and Injustice in a Small Town*. New York: Doubleday.

Groner, Jonathan. (2002). *Lethal Injection: A Stain on the Face of Medicine*, BMJ 325 (7371) 1026-8. https://doi.org/10.1136/bmj.325.7371.1026, published November 2, 2002.

Hatch, Virginia L., Anthony Walsh. (2016). *Capital Punishment: Theory and Practice of the Ultimate Penalty*. Oxford: Oxford University Press.

Huff, Ronald, C., and Martin Killias, eds. (2008). "Wrongful Conviction in the United States." *Wrongful Conviction: International Perspectives on Miscarriages of Justice* 59, 65 (Philadelphia: Temple University Press).

Hunt, S. (2011). "The Admissibility of Eyewitness-Identification Expert Testimony in Oklahoma." *Oklahoma Law Review*, 63, 511–51.

Hunter, Robert S. (1989). *Trial Handbook for Illinois Lawyers: Criminal, 6th ed.* Rochester, NY: Lawyers Cooperative Publishing.

Innocence Project, *Bad Lawyering*, available at http://www.innocenceproject.org/understand/Bad-Lawyering.php, retrieved July 13, 2013.

Innocence Project, *Informants/Snitches*, available at http://www.innocenceproject.org/understand/Snitches-Informants.php, retrieved August 31, 2013.

Innocence Project, *Government Misconduct*, available at http://www.innocenceproject.org/understand/Government-Misconduct.php, retrieved August 4, 2020.

Jones, Vincent R., and Bruce Wilson. (2013). *Innocence and Its Impact on the Reassessment of the Utility of Capital Punishment: Has the Time Come to Abolish the Ultimate Sanction*? 67 U. Miami L.Rev 459, 464–66.

Jones Vincent R., and James R. Coldren, eds. (2011). *The Death Penalty in Focus*. San Diego, Cognella University Readers.

Junkin, Tim. (2004). *Bloodsworth: The True Story of the First Death Row Inmate Exonerated by DNA.* Chapel Hill, NC: Algonquin Books.

Kassin, Saul M. (2008). "False Confessions: Causes, Consequences, and Implications for Reform." 17 *Current Directions in Psychological Science*.

Kassin, Saul M., C.A. Messner, and R.J. Norwick. (2005). "I'd Know a False Confession If I Saw One: A Comparative Study of College Students and Police Investigators." *Law and Human Behavior*, 29.

Kassin, Saul M. (2008). "False Confessions: Causes, Consequences, and Implications for Reform." *Association for Psychological Science*, 17 (4), 248–53.

King, Laura Randa. (1977). *Society's Final Solution: A History and Discussion of the Death Penalty*. Boston: University Press.

Kozinski, Alex, and Sean Gallagher. (1995). "Death: The Ultimate Run-on Sentence." 46 *Case Western Law Review*.

Lippman, Matthew. (2007). *Contemporary Criminal Law: Concepts, Cases, and Controversies.* New York: Sage Publications.

Los Angeles Times, "Death Penalty Costs California $184 Million a Year, Study Says," *LA Times*. June 2, 2011.

Mandery, Evan J. (2011). *Capital Punishment in America: A Balanced Examination*, 2nd ed. Burlington, MA: Jones & Bartlett Learning.

Mandery, Evan J. (2004). "Innocence as a Death Penalty Issue." 40 *Criminal Law Bulletin*.

Marceau, J.F., and H.A. Whitson. (2013). "The Cost of Colorado's Death Penalty." *University of Denver Criminal Law Review*, 3:145–63.

Martelle, Scott. (2021). "California Hated Executions, Now It Should Abolish the Death Penalty." *Los Angeles Times.* December 3.

NBCNews.com. "Colorado Abolishes Capital Punishment," https://nbcnews.com/news/us-news/colorado-abolishes-death-penalty-n1167231.

Neal, Andrea. (1986). "Death Row Inmates Point to Poor Quality of Lawyers Who Defend Them," http://www.latimes.com. October 29, retired March 7, 2021.

Neubauer, David W., and Henry F. Fradella. (2012). *America's Courts and the Criminal Justice System, 11th ed.* Belmont, CA: Wadsworth/Cengage.

New York Times. "Man Executed for 1978 Killing," September 20,1995. www.nytimes.com, retrieved March 20, 2021.

NJADP (New Jersians for Alternatives to the Death Penalty). "The High Cost of New Jersey's Death Penalty." https://www.njadp.org/gadabout&what=cost, retrieved March 25, 2020.

NPR (National Public Radio). "Governor Gavin Newsom Suspends Death Penalty in California," National Public Radio. https://www.npr.org/2019/03/12/702873258/gov-gavin-newsom-suspends-death-penalty-in-california.

Press Release, Illinois Government News Network, "Governor Ryan Declares Moratorium on Executions, Will Appoint Commission to Review Capital Punishment System." January 31, 2000, available at http://www.illinois.gov/PressRelease/PressReleaseListShow.cfm?RecNum=359.

Press Release, Governor Bill Richardson, *Governor Bill Richardson Signs Repeal of the Death Penalty*. March 18, 2009, available at http://www.deathpenaltyinfo.org/document/richardsonstatement.pdf.

Pro Con. 2015. "41 Federal Capital Offenses, Death Penalty." https://pro.con.org/view.resource.php?resourceID=004927, retrieved August 15, 2015.

Riggio, Michael H. (1977). "The Death Penalty History," http://www.cram.com.

Risinger, Michael D. (2007). "Innocents Convicted: An Empirically Justified Factual Wrongful Conviction Rate," 97 *Journal of Criminal Law & Criminology*, 761.

Savage, John. (2018). "The Shocking Legacy of America's Worst Modern-Day Lynching," *Pacific Standard*. June 7–8, 2018, retrieved March 20, 2021.

Sherman, Carter. (2017). "Surviving Bad Lawyers Just Got Tougher for Death Row Inmates." *VICE*. June 28, 2017, http:// www.vice.com, retrieved March 7, 2021.

Smith, Robert T. (2015). "The Worst Lawyers: Death Sentences Are Down Across the Country—Except for Where One of These Guys Is the Defense Attorney." *Slate*. http://www.Slate.com/news-and-politics/2015/11/the-worst-defense-lawyers-for-death-penalty-cases-in-arizona-florida-louisiana.html, retrieved March 1, 2021.

Statistica. (2020). "Total Number of Executions in the United States from 1976 to 2020 by State." http://www.Statista.com, retrieved March 3, 2021.

Statistica. U.S. Capital Punishment—Executions 1976–2020, by Method." Statistica Research Department. https://www.statistica.com.

Steiker, Carol S., and Jordan Steiker. (1995). "Sober Second Thoughts: Reflections on Two Decades of Constitutional Regulation of Capital Punishment," 109 *Harvard Law Review*.

Stull, Brian. (2010). "Good and Bad Lawyers Determine Who Lives and Who Dies." www.ACLU.org. March 10, 2010, retrieved March 7, 2021.

Tempest, Rone. (2005). "Death Row Often Means a Long Life," *LA. Times*. March 6. 2005. http://articles.latimes.com/2005/mar/06/local/me-deathpen6.

Texas Defender Service. (2002). "Lethal Indifference: The Fatal Combination Incompetent Attorneys and Unaccountable Courts in Texas Death Penalty Appeals." Texas Defender Service. http://www.texasdefender.org, retrieved March 1, 2021.

The Death Penalty Information Center, www.deathhpenaltyinfo.org.

The Economist. (2014). "The Death Penalty in California: Cruel and Unusual—A Judge Strikes a Blow Against Capital Punishment." July 26, 2014. https://www.economist.com/news/united-states/21608773-judge-strikes-blow-against-capitalpunishment-cruel-and-unusual.

The New York Times. (1995). "Man Executed for 1978 Killing." September 20,1995, A-18. http://www.nytimes.com, retrieved March 20, 2021.

The University of Miami School of Law Symposium. (2013). "The Future of the Death Penalty in America." 67 *U. Miami L. Rev.* 329.

Walpin, Ned. DPIC, the Death Penalty Information Center. "Why Is Texas #1 Executions?" http://www.dpic.org, retrieved February 19, 2021.

Walters, Dan. (2014). "California Budget Is Balanced? Not by a Long Shot." *Sacramento Bee*. March 30, 2014. http://www.sacbee.com/news/politics-government/dam-walters/article2594117.html.

World Population Review. (2021). "Death Penalty States 2020." https://www.worldpopulationreview.com, retrieved March 16, 2021.

Zalman, Marvin. "Criminal Justice Reform and Wrongful Conviction: A Research Agenda." 17 *Criminal Justice Policy Review*, 2006.

Zalman, M., B. Smith, and A. Kiger. (2008). "Official's Estimates of Incidence of 'Actual Innocence' Convictions," *Justice Quarterly* 25, 72–100.

Index

About the Author

Associate professor **Vincent R. Jones Sr.** is a highly accomplished professor, advocate, and legal scholar. Before becoming a professor, Professor Jones began his legal career as an attorney with the United States Security and Exchange Commission in Chicago. He then worked for several years as a national trial lawyer and was the lead trial attorney on several high-profile cases. As a sought-after public speaker, he has lectured nationally and internationally on such topics as wrongful convictions, death-penalty law and history, international human rights, human trafficking, and terrorism. Professor Jones teaches courses at the doctoral, graduate, and undergraduate levels.

Professor Jones is an advocate for international human rights, the abolition of capital punishment, criminal-justice reform, social-justice advocacy, and solving the problem of wrongful convictions. His book, *The Problem with Capital Punishment*, is his first solo venture.

Education

LLM International Human Rights, Northwestern Pritzker School of Law (2019–present); J.D., University of Illinois, Chicago, School of Law (1988); B.S., Illinois State University, Political Science (1979).

www.ingramcontent.com/pod-product-compliance
Ingram Content Group UK Ltd.
Pitfield, Milton Keynes, MK11 3LW, UK
UKHW041840031026
15587UKWH00002B/913

9 781666 903829